MW00472957

"Brian Borgman has written a v
glorifying book about how to re
paints a biblically accurate pictu
it, 'holy emotions.' It neither di:
This is an important book, and I highly recommend it."

— MARTHA PEACE, biblical counselor; author, *The Excellent Wife*

"What Christian hasn't been confused about the relationship between faith and feelings? In this immensely profitable book, Brian Borgman, a sure-footed guide to this topic, biblically and precisely explains the concept of emotion and how to integrate it into one's walk with the Lord. I know of no other book quite like it. It is scriptural, wise, clear, pastoral, transparent, and compelling. This is a great resource for pastors, counselors, and disciplers. The principles in this work should prove to be of real, lasting value to all believers in Jesus who earnestly yearn to grasp and harness their emotions in the midst of a sensate culture that is quickly careening out of emotional control. We should applaud Pastor Borgman's diligent efforts in bringing us this most helpful volume."

— LANCE QUINN, Senior Pastor, Thousand Oaks Bible Church,
Thousand Oaks, California

"Here is a readable but comprehensive study that unites the Christian's theology and experience. With the heart of a pastor, Brian Borgman offers an emotional lifeline that will stabilize your heart and support your faith. This book needs to be in your personal library. I will return to it time and again—so will you!"

— JANI ORTLUND, author; *His Loving Law, Our Lasting Legacy*

"Brian Borgman has done a lot of work on this crucial topic, and it really shows. Emotion is one of the least understood topics in our Bible studies and churches, and this is a strong contribution to the discussion. I am thankful to have read *Feelings and Faith* and know others will also benefit from it. Brian's heart for God's people shines through clearly on these pages."

— MATTHEW ELLIOTT, author, *Feel: The Power of Listening to
Your Heart*; *Faithful Feelings: Rethinking Emotion in the
New Testament*

"Martin Lloyd-Jones taught us that if we see truth clearly, we must feel it. Authentic faith in the supreme, indomitable goodness of God in sending Jesus Christ as our substitute and redeemer necessarily transforms our feelings. Brian Borgman clearly sets forth the foundational role of truth, unpacks a robust theology of Christian experience, and provides examples of how to mortify sinful emotions and cultivate godly ones. I highly recommend this book."

—ALEX CHEDIAK, associate professor of engineering
and physics, California Baptist University;
author, *With One Voice*

Feelings
and
Faith

Cultivating Godly Emotions in the Christian Life

BRIAN S. BORGMAN

Foreword by Bruce and Jodi Ware

:: CROSSWAY®

WHEATON, ILLINOIS

Feelings and Faith: Cultivating Godly Emotions in the Christian Life

Copyright © 2009 by Brian Steven Borgman

Published by Crossway
    1300 Crescent Street
    Wheaton, Illinois 60187

Cover design: Jon McGrath

First printing 2009

Printed in the United States of America

Trade Paperback ISBN: 978-1-4335-0363-4
ePub ISBN: 978-1-4335-2241-3
PDF ISBN: 978-1-4335-1145-5
Mobipocket ISBN: 978-1-4335-1146-2

Library of Congress Cataloging-in-Publication Data
Borgman, Brian.
 Feelings and faith : cultivating godly emotions in the Christian life
/ Brian S. Borgman ; foreword by Bruce and Jodi Ware.
  p. cm.
 Includes index.
 ISBN 978-1-4335-0363-4 (tpb)
 1. Emotions—Religious aspects—Christianity. I. Title
BV4597.3.B66 2009
233'.5—dc22   2008041694

Crossway is a publishing ministry of Good News Publishers.

CH   28 27 26 25 24 23 22 21 20 19 18

To Ariel,
my wife and best friend.

Because of you, Ecclesiastes 9:9 is a reality in my life.
I love you.

Lioness of God is the meaning of the name
"Ariel," from ancient Hebrew fame.
"Ariel, O Ariel" they called Jerusalem of old,
The city where kings ruled and prophets foretold.

The name of the center of all Israelite life
Is also the name of my God-given wife.
She truly is a woman who is worthy of her name,
Bold in faith, of the Gospel she knows no shame.

The beauty of nature and grace in her are grand,
Making me breathless and grateful as I take her hand;
But it is the beauty of grace that is the sweetest of all
For the beauty of nature like the glory of the flower will fall.

What can I render to God for the treasured wife of my youth?
To praise Him, to cherish her and wash her in His truth,
To enjoy with her this fleeting life, in both pleasure and pain,
And faithfully serve the One who died and rose again.

Like Zion of old, she is no stranger to troubles and trial,
Yet her gaze is fixed, hands on the plough, even with a smile.
Enduring life and ministry, she has learned to kiss the rod.
She is my sweet Ariel, a true lioness of God.

Contents

Foreword

Human emotions—it seems sometimes that you can't live with them, and you can't live without them. How difficult it is to understand just what they are, whether and how they can be regulated, and what role they should play in a healthy Christian's life. Our tendency toward excess can plainly be seen in how we deal with emotions—both ours and others'.

Some among us—call them the rationalists—do their dead-level best to avoid anything bordering on emotion. Reason and logic must guide, they argue, and emotion only threatens to usurp their rightful reign in our lives. But why, then, did God give us the emotions we have? Doesn't this approach seem patently misguided, given the manner in which God both shows forth emotions and calls us also to exhibit strong emotions? It appears that just a bit of reasoning shows the rationalist position on human emotion to be one-sided and reductionist. And yet some quarters of the church are filled with committed rationalists. They often think the Christian faith is little more than correct thinking, and they often reason that the only way to get others to join the Christian faith is to reason them into the kingdom.

Others—call them the emotionalists—do their dead-level best to avoid thinking deeply on just about anything. If, by any chance, some of them have chosen to pick up this book, how they *feel* about what they are encountering will determine whether they decide to read further. They are ruled by the sway of emotional pleasure and pain, running to the former and resisting the latter. But why, then, did God give us our reasoning capacity? Isn't it clear that both biblical teaching and our own experiences show us that following the dictates of emotions can lead to frustration and ruin? And yet some quarters of the church are filled with committed emotionalists. Among such are those who choose a church for how it feels to them, whether it gives them comforting, reassuring, and positive emotional experiences. Truth that disrupts the quest for this positive emotional disposition is viewed as unwelcome and bothersome. So long as they are made to feel good, to laugh at humorous anecdotes or cry at touching stories, to leave feeling happy and contented, they sense that they've been at the right place.

For most of us, the rationalist or emotionalist excess is moderated to some extent. Perhaps it would be correct to say that most Christians have a tendency in one direction or the other, even if they are not dominated by either. Some tend to allow their heads to lead and ignore whether their hearts are engaged, while others tend to follow the lead of emotional longings and suppress the evaluation their minds might be trying to offer. But at least all of us are aware that both head and heart, cognition and emotion, are realities we must reckon with in our experience as human beings and especially as followers of Christ.

Regardless of whether we are in the category of pristine rationalist or emotionalist or somewhere in the middle, nearly all of us could use some help in this area—in fact, many of us could use a lot of help! We need a vision of human personhood that shows just why God made us with the minds and hearts that we have. We need to see the importance of cognition and emotion, of thinking and feeling, of truth and affections, to live out the Christian faith as God intends. We also need to understand the effects of sin on both our heads and our hearts.

What is the relation between truth and feeling? How do I handle emotions of discouragement and despair? Is there a way that truth can affect emotions and emotions affect thinking? Can incorrect thinking bring emotional harm, just as sinful emotions can skew our thinking? Does God give guidance for us on these questions and others like them?

Both of us listened with anticipation to Brian Borgman's sermon series on human emotions, and we were helped greatly through the biblical insight and perception into the human soul these sermons exposed. We have known Brian for a number of years, first as my [Bruce's] student at Western Seminary in Portland, Oregon, and in more recent years as a beloved brother in Christ, friend, and co-laborer in ministry. We have been to his church, and stayed often in Brian and Ariel's home. We have seen the love, respect, and deep appreciation that the people of Grace Community Church extend to him and his family. The members of that church are students of the Word; they come to learn and be fed, and Brian pastors them well. He also loves and leads his family with diligence, joy, and integrity.

So, when we learned that Brian was considering revising his sermon series on emotions for a book, we were delighted. He does a superb job of establishing a firm foundation of biblical truth about emotions and then develops sound teaching regarding the role of our emotions in progressive sanctification. He writes with conviction about the sin in ungodly emotions. And he offers discerning practical advice on how to develop godly emotions through the rich teaching of God's Word and the transforming power of the Spirit. In these emotionally murky times, Brian's book provides a path of clear-sighted guidance and biblical fidelity.

Let the rationalists and emotionalists among us take heart (and mind!). *Feelings and Faith* provides unusual insight and wisdom for growth in holiness through understanding better the crucial role godly emotions play in our lives, as God designed them to do. This book will prove to be a valued resource in personal study, in marriages, in small groups, in Sunday schools, and in other venues. May God be pleased to use *Feelings and Faith* to teach God's people glorious gospel truths to help all find greater balance, depth of personal understanding, and growth in Christlike character—to the praise and glory of God above all.

—*Bruce and Jodi Ware*

Preface

I am a pastor who loves theology. The theological stream I consciously drink from takes doctrine very seriously, something with which I wholeheartedly agree. That's one of the reasons I drink there. My theological tradition (Reformed) puts a great deal of emphasis on the mind. It is a strongly academic tradition and can become very cerebral. So why am I writing a book about the emotions? A few years ago I "felt" the need to teach on the emotions. Since I believe that there is a biblical doctrine of the emotions and am convinced that in our more mind-oriented tradition we could use some perspective on the emotions, I started a "short" sermon series.

I took up the series with enthusiasm. Some in our congregation were a little wary. However, over the years I had put quite a bit of thought into the emotions from a few different angles. John Piper, Jonathan Edwards, and others had furnished much biblical food for me to digest. My own doctoral work on preaching at Westminster Seminary in California had directed me into the specific area of preaching and the emotions, both in the preacher and in the hearers. There was also the steady load of pastoral counseling that had forced on me the necessity of helping people deal biblically with their emotions. It seemed to me that much of what we hear about the emotions is unbiblical and therefore unhelpful. Therefore, I eagerly set out to preach two or three messages on the emotions. Those two or three turned into twenty-two sermons, and I still felt there was more to say!

The sermons aired on Pilgrim Radio, our local Christian radio station. The response was very positive. Our church administrator also added the emotions sermons to our collection on Sermonaudio. com. Over the last few years we have been amazed at how regularly those sermons on the emotions are the highest ranked, according to downloads, in all the sermons we have listed. My fellow elders and our church administrator pressured me, gently and steadily, to get the series in print.

I am personally thankful to the Lord for the number of people who have expressed gratitude for how he has worked through those sermons to bring them much needed help. It was the positive response of our own congregation and the response of listeners over radio and the Internet, which compelled me to put this material in print. It is my hope that God would use what his Word says about the emotions to help more people gain mental and emotional stability and joy rooted in our triune God for his glory.

Who Is This Book For?

This book is practical theology. To my ears, "practical theology" sounds redundant. All theology should be practical and applicable. Many do not see theology that way. My conviction, however, is summed up in what was said about Jonathan Edwards: "All of his doctrine was application and all of his application was doctrine." Practical theology simply should be biblically sound theology, built on good biblical exegesis and exposition, which is then formulated and articulated. In turn, the theological formulation, clearly emerging from the Bible, intersects with real life. The intersection of truth and life is called application. The old-timers would have called it *experimental* or *experiential* religion.

As a result, this book has biblical exposition, theological formulation, and practical application. I have tried to write so that a layman could absorb it with profit (that is how I tried to preach the sermons!). Yet I feel the burden not to hide the exposition or theological processes. The areas that are more technical I will treat in the notes for the sake of fellow pastors and serious Bible and theology students. However, God's people need to be grounded in his Word, so this book is for those who want to explore what God's Word has to say about the emotions and how those truths apply to our lives. This will require some work.

Faith and Feelings: An Overview of the Book

This book has two major parts: foundations and applications. The introduction provides us with two vital pieces of information. First, it briefly exposes the most common misperceptions about the emotions, the cultural clutter of unbiblical thinking. Then it provides a working definition of the emotions that will carry us through the rest of our study. Part 1 is unapologetically theological. Although the notes will take care of some more technical aspects, the biblical and theological foundations cannot be trimmed away for the sake of a "theology-free zone" culture. This section provides a sound theological foundation to build on, without which all would simply be speculation.

Part 2 is also theological, but the emphasis falls on the application of the theology of Part 1. It begins by building a bridge from theology to life through exploring sanctification and our emotions.

The two final parts are specific applications of the theology, focusing on how to put to death ungodly emotions and how to cultivate godly emotions.

Acknowledgments

My human debt of gratitude for the publication of this book begins with Bruce and Jodi Ware. Dr. Ware was my theology professor during Western Seminary days and has been my friend ever since. Bruce and Jodi's encouragement and help continually amaze me. Both are busy servants of the Lord, and yet they took time to help with this project in numerous ways. Jodi's suggestions and corrections were extremely valuable. Ariel and I appreciate both of you very much.

Our friend Rebecca Jones helped me to think about writing as writing and not as preaching. Her insights and suggestions benefited me greatly. Thank you, Rebecca.

I also must thank my friend and our church administrator Gary Wheeler. More than anyone, Gary put gentle and not so gentle pressure on me to get this done. For more than eighteen years now God has knit our hearts together, and we have watched each other grow (and shrink and lose hair).

I also have the privilege of pastoring one of the most wonderful congregations in the church militant, Grace Community Church in Minden, Nevada. They are my family, and I love them, and I love preaching the Word of God to them. We started our life together from scratch in 1993. It has been sweet and tough, but mostly sweet. God has built something real, because it is all about Christ and his Word.

My fellow elders, Dave, Vic, John, Charlie, and Steve, are not only my fellow laborers, but they are also my friends. They are the mantle of credibility to the vital importance of plural eldership. Thank you, brothers.

During the preparation of this manuscript, one of my dear friends and our first deacon, Ernie Kuehnel, went home to be with the Lord. He was a model of faithfulness and emotional stability even during tumultuous times. I miss him.

I would be remiss if I did not thank a host of teachers who have taught me through their writings. It should be obvious that there are many fingerprints all over this work besides mine. I thank God for men like John Piper, Jonathan Edwards, John Owen, Martyn Lloyd-Jones, Paul Tripp, Dietrich Bonhoeffer, Ed Welch, David Powlison, and many more. Matthew Elliott's excellent academic work, *Faithful Feelings*, was not in print when I originally preached the sermon series on which the present volume is based, but it was of inestimable help in later preparation, providing great support and confirmation to my own thinking. Matthew's next book, *Feel*, did not come out until I had finished this manuscript. It is an excellent popular-level work. I thank the Lord for giving these gifts to the body.

The folks at Crossway are incredible. It has been delightful working with them. Thanks to Jill Carter for her efficiency, friendliness, and encouragement. Lydia Brownback has my gratitude. She is an excellent editor. She was always prompt. Her encouragement went far beyond what I expected of an editor. It makes me smile to see her devotionals next to my wife's and daughter's Bibles.

Finally, I want to thank my heavenly Father for a serious and debilitating back injury that happened on the first day of our vacation in the summer of 2007. I also thank him for two weeks of excruciating pain as the interior of the disc strangulated the nerve root in my spinal canal. I also thank him for a successful surgery and for forcing me to stay down for three full months while I healed. It was during this time that he taught me much and gave me the time to write this book. My heavenly Father is perfect in all his ways. I do adore the triune God, who is sovereign and loving.

O Father, You are sovereign, the Lord of human pain,
Transmuting earthly sorrows to gold of heavenly gain.
All evil overruling, as none but Conqu'ror could,
Your love pursues its purpose—our soul's eternal good.

MARGARET CLARKSON

Introduction

She was angry. She was hurt. She was trying unsuccessfully not to cry. Gripping the tissue in her hand like a child's security blanket, she said, "Pastor, you don't understand; you don't know how it feels. The thought of his being with that woman grips my mind like an iron claw and it will not let go. I pray. I cry. I pray again. I do not want to think about it. But I can't help it. The thoughts create a hurricane of emotions. By the time he gets home from work I hate him all over again. I don't want him near me. I want him to die. I can't stand the way I feel."

*　*　*

With a trembling voice that seemed out of place in his massive, rugged frame, he said, "I would wake up and know that God was just waiting to kick sand in my face. If it was a really bad day, I figured God said, 'Forget the sand, I'll just kick your face.' The dark cloud of thinking that God loved other people but certainly did not love me sank me into a deep depression. If something good happened to me, I chalked it up to God playing with me so he could pull the rug out from under me. I believed God hated me, and my feelings would not let me believe anything else."

*　*　*

The pastor said with serious concern, "Scott, I notice you never sing during worship. May I ask why?" With a pseudo-philosophical tone he replied, "You know, I walk into church and see all these people lifting their hands, singing the songs, tears running down their face. Frankly, I am not into all that *emotionalism*. When I come to church I don't think I need to sing, and I certainly don't need to get all 'touchy-feely' with God. After all, you can't trust the emotions, and I am perfectly fine with worshiping God in my own way without all those gushy feelings."

* * *

The defiance was frightening. "I know what you are thinking. I know what you are going to say. But I can tell you right now that nobody has ever loved me like he has. Nobody has ever cared for me and listened to me like he does." The pastor gently yet firmly replied, "But he is not in the Lord; you know what the Word says about being unequally yoked." The rebuttal was undaunted, "I love him, and we are getting married. What do you expect me to do? I'm in love. *I can't help the way I feel.*"

* * *

"Pastor, there is a joy I never knew before. To believe that God really cares about the way I feel and that he has changed the way I feel is amazing to me! I finally get it. God has opened my heart to be compassionate. I care about people. When I sing his praise, I feel a passion for his glory. There is a joy that comes, even when the Word cuts deep. For so many years, I felt emotionally dead to the things of God, but he has breathed something into me. My heart caught up with my head. I finally believe that God has all of me!"

* * *

What do these scenes have in common? It is quite simple. The emotions play a critical role in each person's thinking and behavior.

The unrelenting pain of unforgiveness, the poison of bitterness, the short breaths of anxiety, the cancer of lust, the devastation of volcanic anger, the ravages of insane jealousy, the inescapable ruts that lead to strife and broken relationships, habitual patterns that drag one into depression all have one thing in common: they are all related to our emotions.

The tears of joy while singing God's praise, the conviction of sin during the preaching of the Word, the contentment that comes from holding your wife as you watch the sunset, the thrill that comes from seeing your son hit a home run during All-Stars, the satisfaction of a good day's work, and the sense of peace that flows from communion with God are also all related to our emotions. Matthew Elliott does not overstate the case when he says, "Everything we do, say, and think is, in some sense, emotional. We enjoy it, we dislike it, or we just don't care. We describe our experiences and ourselves by describing how we feel. Life without emotions would be in black and white."[1]

But what can we do about the emotions? This is a huge question for me because as a pastor I am called to help people. I want to see them mature into Christlikeness and practical godliness. My desire is that they grow into mighty oaks of righteousness as moms and dads, husbands and wives, sons and daughters, employers and employees, followers of Jesus in a hostile world. As a result, I need to help people deal with anger, lust, bitterness, and envy and grow in faith, joy, peace, and contentment. If I do not see that the emotions play a crucial role in all of life, then I am a blind guide. Martyn Lloyd-Jones observed:

> I regard it as a great part of my calling in the ministry to emphasize the priority of the mind and the intellect in connection with the faith; but though I maintain that, I am equally ready to assert that the feelings, the emotions, the sensibilities obviously are of very vital importance. We have been made in such a way that they play a dominant part of our make-up. Indeed, I suppose that one of the greatest problems in our life in this world, not only for Christians, but for all people, is the right handling of our feelings and emotions. Oh, the havoc that is wrought and the tragedy, the misery and the wretchedness that are to be found in the world simply because people do not know how to handle their own feelings! Man is so constituted that the feelings are in this very prominent position, and indeed, there is a very good case for saying that perhaps the final thing which regeneration and the new birth do for us is just to put the mind and the emotions and the will in their right positions.[2]

Have you ever wondered why so many of God's people stay stuck as stunted saplings instead of growing into mighty oaks in the Lord? Why is it that people who attend good Bible-teaching churches with sound doctrine often fail to progress, even though well taught? Why do certain sins cling like sap from an evergreen, while certain fruits of the Spirit barely dangle from the branch? I propose that one of the reasons is that we do not have a biblical understanding of our emotions, and therefore there is little or no biblical handling of the emotions. We try to treat symptoms and fail to get to the root of the matter.

We are under a twofold obligation to understand our emotions. First, the emotions are a biblical subject. Since the Bible has much to say about the emotions, it is imperative for us to understand what it teaches. Whenever God speaks, on whatever subject he addresses, we are obliged to listen and learn. Second, the emotions are a deeply personal subject, playing a prominent role in each of our lives. Therefore, it is vital to understand what the Bible has to say for our own personal maturity.

It is only when we gain a biblical perspective on this significant part of our humanity that we can begin to grow and put the mind and the emotions and the will in their right positions. As we learn to understand and handle our emotions biblically, we begin to mature in new ways. My pastoral experience has taught me that a biblical understanding of the emotions and the application of these truths can become a virtual greenhouse for spiritual growth and maturity.

If our emotions are to be sanctified, if our emotions are to be conformed to the image of Christ, then we must have a grasp on what the Bible says. If we are going to successfully cultivate our emotions for greater godliness and put to death those destructive, ungodly emotions, then we must have a handle on what the Bible says about them. A biblical theology is foundational for us if we ever hope to understand our emotions and grow spiritually. A commitment to the sufficiency of Scripture must undergird our approach. A confidence in the grace of God is a prerequisite if we are to change. Once that commitment and confidence are firmly in place, we can begin the journey with the expectation that God will teach us, prune us, and grow us.

As soon as we start this journey, however, we encounter

obstacles and potential detours because there is so much erroneous teaching on the emotions. We need to navigate around the obstacles, avoiding dangerous detours, and cut a clear course when it comes to the emotions and what the Bible teaches. To think erroneously, that is, unbiblically, about the emotions is to be held captive by wrong thinking and to remain powerless to overcome wrong feelings and cultivate right feelings. To have a biblical foundation for understanding the emotions is to think rightly about them. Such an understanding is a *pou sto*, a place to stand. To have a theologically robust perspective on the proper use of the emotions is to enter into the greenhouse of spiritual growth, for, as Jonathan Edwards argued in his classic, *Religious Affections*, "The nature of true religion consists in holy affections."

Common Misconceptions about the Emotions

Our secular culture is preoccupied with emotional wholeness. We are a therapeutic society in search of wellness. Take for instance the support group Emotions Anonymous. Their Web site reads:

> Emotions Anonymous is a twelve-step organization, similar to Alcoholics Anonymous. Our fellowship is composed of people who come together in weekly meetings for the purpose of working toward recovery from emotional difficulties. EA members are from many walks of life and are of diverse ages, economic status, social and educational backgrounds. The only requirement for membership is a desire to become well emotionally.[3]

The number of self-help books, seminars, CDs, DVDs, institutes, and gurus of inner peace and emotional wholeness is overwhelming. The foundational perspective of any given book or seminar may vary from a minimal foundation, just dealing with emotions as something we feel, to an evolutionary psychology of the emotions that is purely physiological and chemical. But apart from Christian theology there is no sound understanding of the emotions. Yet many Christians, influenced by our psychologized culture, fall prey to the shallow, even godless, views of the emotions.

Some Christians teach that emotions are bad and need to be suppressed. From the philosophical side of life Plato, Aristotle, and the Stoics argued that passions (emotions) could not coexist with moral virtue. Emotions are contrary to reason and all rational principles, thus they are contrary to all that is desirable and good. Therefore, moral virtue includes the subduing of the emotions. A common Christian version of this says that the mind is all that is important. The emotions do nothing but mess us up. They cannot be trusted and should be suppressed. A stoic and cerebral Christianity is the result.

Others have not gone that far but do teach that the emotions are irrelevant and unnecessary. What matters is not feeling but believing or doing. The emotions are there, but they are like in-laws who have overstayed their welcome; they are a nuisance and best if ignored. This view of the emotions is captured in a gospel tract:

> Let's say that a snowmobile represents "fact" and the sled it is pulling represents "feelings." *A snowmobile will run fine without a sled.* And, of course, it would be useless for a sled to try to pull a snowmobile. It is the same way when we are Christians. We cannot trust our feelings. We have to put our trust in God.

It is certainly true that we put our trust in God and not in our feelings. But the message is clear: the emotions are optional. They are untrustworthy. Our faith would function fine without them.

Another misconception about the emotions that many Christians buy into is that emotions are so powerful that they govern and control us. At the popular level this is seen in expressions such as "I can't help the way I feel!" This appeal to the sovereignty of the emotions is used to justify hatred, divorce, infidelity, and all kinds of sinful conduct. From this perspective, the emotions remain immune from obedience, exempt from Christ's lordship; they are simply external forces that thrust themselves upon us, leaving us at their mercy. One Christian writer expresses this sentiment: "As a saved person, you can control your mind and your will, but not your feelings. God's plan is for us to *believe* Him and choose to submit ourselves to His loving care and authority regardless of how we feel. All together now, *Rain on how I feel!*"[4]

Just as some Christians elevate reason and dismiss the emotions, others believe that the emotions are the most important thing about us. This view or, rather, *feeling* turns many Christians into experience junkies who just want to have an emotional high. Such experiences are the sum and substance of their Christianity. They reduce their faith to an empty emotionalism. Being led by the Spirit is nothing more than how a person feels about something. Feelings determine duty. Doctrine is determined by "how I feel about it," thus, "I don't believe *that* doctrine because it makes me feel yucky." The idea that the emotions should be changed, sanctified, or cultivated is not even on the radar.

This is a very brief and generalized view of some of the most common misconceptions about the emotions. Although these are generalizations, they are accurate ones.

A Working Definition of the Emotions

The Bible does not give us a clinical definition of the emotions, but it does give us numerous words that describe both the source and expression of the emotions. The Bible often commands our feelings, commending or condemning certain emotions. This is an important observation in establishing a working definition. In the Bible, emotions are not amoral. We are responsible for how we feel, and we are expected to exercise self-control and have certain emotions.

Matthew Elliott's thorough work on the emotions goes into great detail answering the question, "What is emotion?"[5] Historically, there are two views on the emotions: one sees the emotions as unrelated to the mind or thinking (the noncognitive view). The other sees the emotions directly related to the mind or thinking (the cognitive view). For those interested in the philosophical and psychological nuances I gladly point you to Elliott's excellent work. The noncognitive view is generally an evolutionary perspective that sees emotions as a physiological change in feeling (e.g., sweaty palms, racing heart, euphoria), which is named by the person experiencing the change (fear, happiness, etc.). In other words, we are subject to our emotions and are not ultimately responsible for them. They are something that happens to us, physically or chemically. We cry and feel sadness. We feel anxiety because our hearts race. Although emotions often have physiological manifestations (the Bible affirms this), this view is biblically unacceptable. It also flies in the face of common sense and is just plain backwards!

The cognitive view of the emotions sees the emotions as based on beliefs, standards, judgments, evaluations, concerns, and thoughts. The emotions and reason are interdependent. The emotions are not simply impulses; they are the indicators of what we value and what we believe. "Our emotions can be considered to arise from our beliefs and concerns."[6] The emotions reflect and express the inner man, the heart, the soul, the mind. They have an object. For instance, thinking about anger cannot make us angry, but thinking about the injustice of abortion can make us angry. The object of the emotion of anger is the injustice of abortion because we value human life. The thought of losing one's spouse can cause us fear or sorrow. The emotion of fear has an object: the thought of losing a spouse. Seeing my daughter deliver the valedictorian speech at her graduation brings me joy, because I value my daughter and am proud of her achievement. The power of the emotion is based on our own personal evaluation and valuing of the object. I would have a different emotional response seeing a car hit a jackrabbit and a car hitting a child. Matthew Elliott summarizes this:

> Emotions are not primitive impulses to be controlled or ignored, but cognitive judgments or construals that tell us about ourselves and our world. In this understanding, destructive motives can be changed, beneficial emotions can be cultivated, and emotions are a crucial part of morality. Emotions also help us to work efficiently, assist our learning, correct faulty logic and help us build relationships with others.[7]

As we work through the theology of the emotions, we will do so using this definition: *the emotions are an inherent part of what it means to be a person; they express the values and evaluations of a person and influence motives and conduct.*[8] The emotions are more than feelings;

they tell us about what we value and what we believe, producing desires and inclinations that affect our behavior. "Emotions were given in order to energize behavior and were intended by God to be a catalyst for action."[9]

This does not mean that all emotions are rational. They often are not. But it does identify the fact that the emotions are responses to our perceptions, which may be right or wrong, real or imagined. "Emotions are the language of the soul. They are the cry that gives the heart a voice."[10] This is not to claim that all emotions are easily intelligible and able to be thoroughly analyzed. They often cannot. And yet, we must learn to understand this basic part of our humanity. Sam Williams rightly notes, "God gives emotions for a specific purpose. They are necessary for us properly to know and relate to and glorify God."[11]

Part One

A Biblical-theological Foundation for Understanding Our Emotions

CHAPTER 1

The Character of God

The child, the philosopher, and the religionist have all one question: "What is God like?"
At the outset I must acknowledge that this question cannot be answered except to say that
God is not like anything; that is, He is not exactly like anything or anybody.

A. W. TOZER[1]

We begin our biblical-theological foundation with the starting point of all true theology—God. The theology that does not begin with God will end in error. God is the beginning, middle, and end of all things (Rom. 11:36). In the Bible God displays a variety of emotions. We could even say that emotions are part of his divine nature or person. Matthew Elliott straightforwardly asserts, "It is clear that the Old Testament presents Yahweh as an emotional God. . . . God's emotions play a key role in many texts, as God feels with intensity."[2] This is an important yet neglected area of the doctrine of God. It is, as Pastor Greg Nichols says, "uncharted water."

The unambiguous biblical portrayal of God is that he has absolute capacity to feel and has perfectly holy emotions. In the history of systematic theology, the mind and will of God have often been the focus. But the Bible speaks of God's heart, his emotions and feelings. Some circles deny that God actually has emotions. This is called the doctrine of divine impassibility.[3] However, the sheer weight of biblical evidence demands that we see God as a being who has real emotions and feels intensely. Nichols defines God's emotional capacity:

> God's emotivity is His supreme capacity to act responsively and sensationally; to feel pure and principled affections of love and hate, joy and grief, pleasure and anger, and peace; in accord with His supreme, spiritual, and simple Being and impeccable virtue.[4]

Immediately we must qualify our statements on God's emotions for the simple reason that we cannot experientially relate to this dimension of God because we are so different. The real danger is to impose our emotional experiences on God and thus be guilty of the indictment of Psalm 50:21, "You thought I was just like you" (HCSB). We must keep in mind that God's emotional capacities are both invulnerable and perfect. His emotions are not dependent on anything outside of himself. Although he responds to and is moved by human events, he is never emotionally vulnerable, never surprised by an event or overcome with emotion. His feelings are not subject to sinfulness, since he is holy. His emotions are perfectly righteous in their essence and exhibition. Elliott again notes, "God's emotions are always in line with His holiness and moral character. God's emotions are always correct, righteous and moral because He is always correct, righteous and moral."[5]

The legendary Princeton theologian Benjamin B. Warfield has captured the importance of recognizing God's emotions: "A God without an emotional life would be a God without all that lends its highest dignity to personal spirit, whose very being is movement; and that is as much as to say no God at all."[6]

Throughout the whole Bible, we see a God who has and expresses perfect emotions. We cannot cover all of them, but we will expound some of them and, hopefully, in the process see God more clearly in the light of his Word.

God Loves and Delights in His Son

The emotions God has for his Son are experienced by us in small, reflective ways when we have children of our own. There is that innate sense of joy we have as we look at or hold that little one. There is a real delight that wells up within us as we watch their achievements, whether those be in sports, school, music, or the arts. There is a pride that can fill our hearts when we see our children do the right thing, treat someone kindly, or make a sacrifice for the greater good. All of these emotions, and infinitely more, are in God as he explicitly and perfectly loves and delights in his own Son.

In Isaiah 42:1, Yahweh says, "Behold my servant, whom I

uphold, my chosen, in whom my soul delights; I have put my Spirit upon him; he will bring forth justice to the nations." In this first Servant Song from Isaiah,[7] the Father identifies the Messiah as his servant and his chosen. He is the one who is in subjection to the will of the Father and the one who will fulfill the purpose of the Father. Then the Father says that his soul *delights* in this chosen servant. The Hebrew word (*ratzah*) denotes a sense of being pleased with, taking delight or pleasure in. It is truly hard to imagine how this inter-Trinitarian language could be stripped of emotion. The text compels us to see that the Father infinitely values his Son. The text reverberates with his feelings of pleasure in his Son, who humbled himself in the incarnation to manifest the love of his Father and fulfill his purpose.

At the beginning of our Lord's earthly ministry and at the very end we have bookends of the Father's unbounded delight in his Son. At Jesus' baptism we read, "Behold, a voice from heaven said, 'This is my beloved Son, with whom I am well pleased'" (Matt. 3:17). In our Lord's High Priestly Prayer we hear him say, "Father, I desire that they also, whom you have given me, may be with me where I am, to see my glory that you have given me *because you loved me before the foundation of the world*" (John 17:24). John Piper has beautifully stated,

> We may conclude that the pleasure of God in His Son is pleasure in Himself. Since the Son is the image of God, and indeed *is* God, therefore God's delight in the Son is delight in Himself. The original, the primal, the deepest, the foundational joy of God is the joy He has in His own perfections as He sees them reflected in the glory of His Son. Paul speaks of "the glory of God in the face of Christ" (2 Corinthians 4:6). From all eternity God has beheld the panorama of His own perfections in the face of His Son. All that He is He sees reflected fully and perfectly in the countenance of His Son. And in this He rejoices with infinite joy.[8]

God Delights in Justice and Righteousness

After the trial and execution of one of the most ruthless dictators of the modern world, I told my family, "Justice was done and we ought to give thanks." Why give thanks at something as gruesome as that? The reason is that Yahweh delights in justice and righteousness. He delights when his creatures demonstrate it. When a court hands down a just verdict, when a judge delivers a righteous sentence, when a man does a just act or a righteous deed, God is pleased. He loves justice because he is just. He loves righteousness because he is righteous. He has a passion for justice and righteousness. When his creatures reflect something of his character by exercising justice and righteousness, he delights in and loves such displays.

Psalmists and prophets echo this theme repeatedly. "He loves righteousness and justice; the earth is full of the steadfast love of the LORD" (Ps. 33:5). "For I the LORD love justice; I hate robbery and wrong; I will faithfully give them their recompense, and I will make an everlasting covenant with them" (Isa. 61:8). "But let him who boasts boast in this, that he understands and knows me, that I am the LORD who practices steadfast love, justice, and righteousness in the earth. For in these things I delight, declares the LORD" (Jer. 9:24). This both resonates with and scares us.

God Rejoices in His People

If we are listening, we constantly hear notes about how worthy we are, how we really are "all that" and a whole lot more. The notes play repeatedly in Christian books, sermons, and music. Our Christian pop music overflows with unbiblical perspectives on how worthy we are. There is a shallow, sentimental, "It's all about me" mentality. However, in our reaction to this unbiblical emphasis, wanting to underscore human depravity and wickedness, we may end up missing an important truth about how God feels about his people. God actually values and rejoices in his people, not because of who we are in ourselves, but because of what he has made us by his grace. In the words of Casting Crowns:

> Not because of who I am, but because of what You've done.
> Not because of what I've done, but because of who You are.[9]

Listen to the language of love and passion welling up within God:

For as a young man marries a young woman,
      so shall your sons marry you,
and as the bridegroom rejoices over the bride,
      so shall your God rejoice over you. (Isa. 62:5)

The LORD your God is in your midst,
      a mighty one who will save;
he will rejoice over you with gladness;
      he will quiet you by his love;[10]
he will exult over you with loud singing. (Zeph. 3:17)

"I will give them one heart and one way, that they may fear me forever, for their own good and the good of their children after them. I will make with them an everlasting covenant, that I will not turn away from doing good to them. And I will put the fear of me in their hearts, that they may not turn from me. I will rejoice in doing them good, and I will plant them in this land in faithfulness, with all my heart and all my soul." (Jer. 32:39–41)

The language in these texts soars with emotion. When God wants to communicate how he feels about his people, he puts it in terms that are already emotionally percolating for us. The groom sees the bride; his heart leaps within, racing with excitement. He expresses his passionate delight in his people with words such as "rejoice over you with gladness." He paints the picture of being quiet over us with his love, as a parent lovingly yet quietly looks at his child. God goes from quietness to loud, joyful singing. Imagine, God singing for joy over his people! Jeremiah uses "all my heart and all my soul." The language throbs with emotional imagery, capturing God's deep feelings for his people.

God Takes Pleasure in Himself, His Ways, His Grace, and His People's Obedience

Psalmists, sages, and apostles celebrate these pleasures of God. "Our God is in the heavens; he does all that he pleases" (Ps. 115:3). "When a man's ways please the LORD, he makes even his enemies to be at peace with him" (Prov. 16:7). "I have received full payment, and more. I am well supplied, having received from Epaphroditus the gifts you sent, a fragrant offering, a sacrifice acceptable and pleasing to God" (Phil. 4:18; see also 1 Thess. 4:1). "[He] predestined us to adoption as sons by Jesus Christ to Himself, according to the good pleasure of His will" (Eph. 1:5, NKJV).

God takes pleasure in his own will. What he wills to do pleases him, and what pleases him he wills to do. He delights in the obedience and generosity of his people as a reflection of his own grace. He took pleasure in freely adopting his children into his family, apart from any virtue in them. Again, the pleasure is the emotion of joy and delight in doing his will, demonstrating his sovereign grace and seeing his grace at work in his people. God is indeed the blessed God (1 Tim. 1:11). He is the eternally joyful, authentically happy God, who overflows with delight in his own perfections as they are perfectly reflected in his Son and imperfectly and dimly reflected in his creatures.

God Grieves and Experiences Pain and Sorrow

Just as God has joyful feelings, he also has emotions of grief, sadness, sorrow, and even pain. These emotions need to be qualified of course, but there is no need to relegate them to mere figures of speech.[11] We cannot miss the depth of feeling in these passages. The unrestrained depravity at the time of Noah grieved God:

> The LORD saw that the wickedness of man was great in the earth, and that every intention of the thoughts of his heart was only evil continually. And the LORD was sorry that he had made man on the earth, and it grieved him to his heart. (Gen. 6:5–6)

Even when his own people were on the rebellion treadmill, his love for them flowed over in a parental grief. "They put away the foreign gods from among them and served the LORD; and He could bear the misery of Israel no longer" (Judg. 10:16, NASB). The father heart of God is unveiled repeatedly: "How often they rebelled against him in the wilderness and grieved him in the desert!" (Ps. 78:40). "Again and again they tempted God, and pained the Holy One of Israel" (Ps. 78:41, NASB). Just so God appeals to his people through Paul: "Do not grieve the Holy Spirit of God, by whom you were sealed for the day of redemption" (Eph. 4:30; cf. Isa. 63:10).

There are also numerous texts where God expresses his grief and pain in terms of a husband whose heart has been broken by an unfaithful wife, for example, in Ezekiel 6:9: "I have been broken over their whoring heart that has departed from me and over their eyes that go whoring after their idols."[12] Those who have suffered the awful reality of knowing that their spouse has been with someone else sexually will immediately recognize that the language God chooses carries with it the deepest emotional pain. As a pastor, I have seen the endless stream of tears and the trembling hands and have heard the quivering voice of a soul shattered into a million pieces because that one-flesh union has been violated. Another person, an outsider, has been in that sacred place reserved by vow and covenant only for the spouse. It is a violent violation. It is a cruel act, which goes far beyond the anatomy of intercourse. It is crushing. God uses this very language to give us a picture into his heart.

In these passages, God is grieved. He expresses sorrow, even pain. He comes to a point where he can no longer bear the misery of his people. He is grieved over his covenant people's rebellion. He is devastated by their infidelity. He is wounded as they give him a vote of no confidence in the wilderness. This language does not take away from God's sovereignty or immutability. To interpret these emotional terms in such a way that detracts from or nullifies his sovereignty or foreknowledge is to violate the whole counsel of God. Nevertheless, to interpret these strong emotional words as figures of speech with no emotional reality is to drain them of their meaning and force. The God of the Bible knows what it is to sorrow and grieve.

God Experiences Anger, Wrath, and Detestation

Anger management is in. Blow your cork at work and you will find yourself in a class designed to help people control their anger.

Although anger is a common and harmful sin, anger in and of itself is not sinful. In fact, our capacity to be angry is a reflection of the image of God in us. Unfortunately, we rarely know righteous anger. Thankfully, righteous anger is the only anger God knows.

God demonstrates his righteous care for the underprivileged by becoming angry when they are oppressed: "You shall not mistreat any widow or fatherless child. If you do mistreat them, and they cry out to me, I will surely hear their cry, and my wrath will burn, and I will kill you with the sword, and your wives shall become widows and your children fatherless" (Ex. 22:22–24).

He does not hide his detestation for evildoers, liars, and the violent. "The boastful shall not stand before your eyes; you hate all evildoers. You destroy those who speak lies; the LORD abhors the bloodthirsty and deceitful man" (Ps. 5:5–6). "God is a righteous judge, and a God who feels indignation every day" (Ps. 7:11).

His hatred of certain sins is something he refuses to hold close to his vest:

> *For forty years I loathed that generation*
> *and said, "They are a people who go astray in their heart,*
> *and they have not known my ways." (Ps. 95:10)*

> *There are six things that the LORD hates,*
> *seven that are an abomination to him:*
> *haughty eyes, a lying tongue,*
> *and hands that shed innocent blood,*
> *a heart that devises wicked plans,*
> *feet that make haste to run to evil,*
> *a false witness who breathes out lies,*
> *and one who sows discord among brothers. (Prov. 6:16–19)*

"For I hate divorce," says the LORD, the God of Israel, "and him who covers his garment with wrong," says the LORD of hosts. "So take heed to your spirit, that you do not deal treacherously." (Mal. 2:16, NASB)

Even as God loves justice, so he despises injustice, especially injustice done to the helpless of society: the widows, orphans, and unjustly divorced wives. There are certain sins for which God has a special hatred. As a holy God he also has a perfect loathing of evildoers and those who are willfully ignorant and will not trust him. Although there is a biblical doctrine of God's universal love, it should not be too hard to understand that the God of perfection is a complex being who transcends our ability to comprehend. That God can love and hate the same object at the same time is a reflection of his incomprehensibility and emotional complexity. "God does not love the sinner and is angry at the sin. Rather, God loves the sinner and is angry at the sinner when he sins."[13] All theological nuances aside, the words used in these texts pulsate with the emotion of anger.

God Is Compassionate

My wife surpasses me in a multitude of Christian graces and virtues. She is far more spiritual than I am. One of the graces in which she surpasses me is compassion. Although there have been many times when I have felt pity for someone who was in a dire situation, my wife seems to have a consistent sense of compassion that compels her to action again and again. In this, she is much more like her heavenly Father than I am. It is beautiful. The Bible does indeed celebrate God's compassion:

> "I will make all my goodness pass before you and will proclaim before you my name 'The Lord.' And I will be gracious to whom I will be gracious, and will show mercy on whom I will show mercy." (Ex. 33:19)

> *As a father shows compassion to his children,*
> *so the Lord shows compassion to those who fear him. (Ps. 103:13)*

> *"Can a woman forget her nursing child,*
> *that she should have no compassion on the son of her womb?*
> *Even these may forget,*
> *yet I will not forget you.*
> *Behold, I have engraved you on the palms of my hands;*
> *your walls are continually before me." (Isa. 49:15–16)*

The Hebrew word *racham*, used in each of the above passages and often translated "show mercy," is the word for *compassion*. It is a word of intense feeling and deep tenderness. It is a gut-level word, communicating a depth of emotion. This depth of feeling is vividly painted for us in the Isaiah passage. The Lord uses the deepest attachment known by humans, a mother and her nursing child. A nursing child derives its very life from its mother. The bond is almost mystical. This is a transcultural experience. It is universal. The bond between mother and child is the most fundamental, affectionate, tender, inviolable bond we know. And yet "the love of the Lord transcends in permanence the best earth can offer."[14]

God Is Loving

God's love obviously relates to his compassion. However, there is a unique emphasis in the Bible on God's love. It is the love of God that is most closely connected to the gospel itself.

> *The LORD appeared to him from far away.*
> *I have loved you with an everlasting love;*
> *therefore I have continued my faithfulness to you. (Jer. 31:3)*

> *Who is a God like you, pardoning iniquity*
> *and passing over transgression*
> *for the remnant of his inheritance?*
> *He does not retain his anger forever,*
> *because he delights in steadfast love.*
> *He will again have compassion on us;*
> *he will tread our iniquities underfoot.*
> *You will cast all our sins*
> *into the depths of the sea.*
> *You will show faithfulness to Jacob*
> *and steadfast love to Abraham,*
> *as you have sworn to our fathers*
> *from the days of old. (Mic. 7:18–20)*

And of course the most famous verse in all of the Bible:

For God so loved the world, that he gave his only Son, that whoever believes in him should not perish but have eternal life. (John 3:16)

We do a grave disservice to God when we say his love has nothing to do with feelings or the emotions. We diminish the dignity of God's person when we unwittingly relegate love to mere actions of goodwill or self-sacrifice. Such a definition of love is absolutely excluded by 1 Corinthians 13:3. The Bible condemns noble, altruistic deeds apart from love, so how can love simply be noble deeds apart from feelings? God's love has a strong emotional element to it. Whatever fragmented notes of beautiful feelings may be found in our love, these are merely distant echoes of the thunderous symphony of God's love.

This is a very brief survey, but the texts speak for themselves. They are a powerful testimony to the emotions of God. This is a significant theological foundation, which has important ramifications. God is not a static being (immutability does not mean static); he is a dynamic, personal being, possessing within himself perfect knowledge, a perfect will, and perfect emotions. He loves, he hates, and he rejoices. He is pleased, displeased, grieved, and angered. He has compassion, love, and pleasure. He interacts with and responds to his people within the framework of both a sovereign decree and perfect emotions, which reflect his values and evaluations, and influence his conduct toward them.

We are made in the image and likeness of God. In order for us to understand ourselves, we must understand God. Although there is an infinite distance between the transcendent, majestic, exalted God and us, his creatures, we can look to God and see the perfect, eternal one who possesses the glorious capacity to feel. In that capacity, he shows the dignity of his person and that we were made not only to think and do but also to *feel*. "Emotions are a good and legitimate part of man's character because they are clearly part of God's character."[15]

The Character of the Living Word and the Written Word

The Lord Jesus Christ is God in human flesh. He is the Word who became flesh (John 1:14). The Bible teaches us that Jesus Christ is the perfect reflection of his Father and of the divine nature. The apostle Paul says, "He is the image of the invisible God" (Col. 1:15; cf. 2 Cor. 4:4), and, "in him the whole fullness of deity dwells bodily" (Col. 2:9). The writer to the Hebrews states the same truth: "He is the radiance of the glory of God and the exact imprint of his nature" (Heb. 1:3). Is it any wonder that our Lord Jesus said to Philip, "Whoever has seen me has seen the Father" (John 14:9)?

The Character of the Living Word: Jesus Christ

When the second Person of the eternal Godhead became man, he became man in a way that reflected his deity. So when our Lord Jesus showed emotion or expressed his feelings, we can assume that what was exhibited was in perfect harmony with his deity. However, in the incarnation Jesus is also perfect humanity, without sin or defect. This means not only is there a reflection of the divine nature in Jesus' emotions but also that the Lord Jesus had a perfect emotional makeup (constitution) and perfect emotional expressions. B. B. Warfield, in a must-read article, said, "It belongs to the truth of our Lord's humanity that he was subject to all sinless emotions."[1]

If our view of the emotions is skewed to begin with (see "Common Misconceptions about the Emotions" [23–25], then we end up missing this glorious aspect of our Lord's person and the rich example he is to us. To say, as one author does, that "Jesus

Christ could not control His emotions when He walked planet earth"[2] is not only to blaspheme the flawless character of our Lord, but to rob God's people of the beauty and example of our Lord's emotional life. When we fix our eyes on Jesus, we see a variety of emotions, perfectly reflecting his Father as well as his own full deity and perfect humanity. When later in the book we get to cultivating godly emotions, we will examine in more detail Jesus' emotional life and how it serves as a pattern for us. For now, the character of Christ stands as another biblical and theological pillar for understanding our emotions. If Christ, perfect God and perfect man, had and displayed perfect emotions, then we must pay special attention. "Whoever says he abides in him ought to walk in the same way in which he walked" (1 John 2:6).

The Character of the Written Word: The Holy Bible

The Holy Scripture is God-breathed (2 Tim. 3:16). When the biblical writers communicated, they were being infallibly carried along by the Holy Spirit (2 Pet. 1:21). We have God's revelation to us in the Bible. God is communicating with us in the Bible. How someone communicates tells us much about that person. How he communicates also shows how he expects his listeners to respond. Watch somebody speak about something that is deeply meaningful to him. Watch him when the listener responds. If the response is indifference, his reaction may be frustration or even anger. But if the response is interest, he will feel that he has effectively communicated the message.

When God speaks to us in his Word, he does not give us simple, straightforward propositional truth statements. The Bible does not read like a legal brief. God's Word is certainly truth (John 17:17), and there are propositional statements, but it is not a series of doctrinal theses. God communicates with passion and emotion in his Word, and such communication is designed to make us respond in like manner.

Much of the Bible was written not merely to inform us but to move us. "Scripture not only speaks about emotions, it also speaks to and through our emotions. The Bible itself is emotional literature, filled with emotional expression and designed not just to communicate with our rationality but also to stir us emotionally, thus affirming our emotionality."[3]

God tells us stories; most of his Word is in narrative. When we read the story of Joseph and finally get to Genesis 45, where we find that Joseph could no longer control himself before his brothers and so cried out, "I am your brother, Joseph, whom you sold into Egypt," we weep with Joseph! When we read the story of Absalom's death and we hear the cry of his father, David—"O my son Absalom, my son, my son Absalom! Would I had died instead of you, O Absalom, my son, my son!"—our hearts break with David's. God communicates in a way that grips the heart and moves the emotions.

Even in the prophetic portions of Scripture, God speaks in a way that touches the heart. For instance, God says in Isaiah 65:2, "I spread out my hands all the day to a rebellious people, who walk in a way that is not good, following their own devices." Why not just say this in theological language: "I have sent forth the general call, which can be resisted, not the effectual call, which cannot be resisted"? Why use the vivid language of stretching out his hands all day long? Why use language that portrays pleading and imploring? The language is designed to reflect the heart of God and move our hearts.

How many times does God use the provocative language of adultery in the Prophets? Are those sections lacking in detail? Doesn't God himself take one of the most painful human experiences, infidelity in marriage, and apply it to himself and to his relationship with his people in graphically emotional ways? God presents himself as the jilted lover, whose heart is broken. He says in Hosea 11:8, "My heart is turned over within Me" (NASB). God presents the sins of his people in the sickening and tragic images of an adulterous woman who will sleep with any man. It is vivid, descriptive, emotional language, not simply designed to inform but to move. God wants us to *feel* the truth.

Jonathan Edwards identified this aspect of God's Word in his own Edwardsean way:

If we ought to exercise our affections at all, they ought to be exercised about those objects which are most worthy of them. But is there anything which Christians can find in heaven or on earth so worthy to be the objects of their admiration and love, their earnest and longing desires, their hope, and their rejoicing, and their fervent zeal, as those things that are held forth to us in the gospel of Jesus Christ? In the Gospels, things are declared which are most worthy to affect us, *but they also are exhibited in the most affecting manner.* The glory and beauty of the blessed Jehovah, which is most worthy in itself to be the object of our admiration and love, *is there exhibited in the most affecting manner that can be conceived of,* as it appears shining in all its luster in the face of an incarnate, infinitely loving, meek, compassionate dying Redeemer. All the virtues of the Lamb of God, His humility, patience, meekness, submission, obedience, love and compassion, *are exhibited before us in a manner that is most tending to move our affections.* . . . God has revealed the affairs of our redemption, through His glorious dispensations, in a purposeful way, designing it in such a manner as to have the greatest possible tendency to reach our heart, and move our affections, most sensibly and strongly. How great cause have we therefore to be humbled to the dust that we are no more affected![4]

Conclusion

The God of the Bible feels intensely. His Son, as the perfect reflection of deity and the perfect embodiment of humanity, felt deeply. As God communicates in his own holy and inspired Word, he seeks to teach, to inform, and to move us earnestly. In light of these truths, we ought to learn to better understand and handle our emotions.

Once these biblical truths make an impact, we start to realize that our emotional state is an important part of us. No longer can we make excuses about our feelings or lack of feelings; there is a biblical mandate to further explore this part of our humanity. This might be scary; our emotions can expose things about us that we may not like or want to deal with. The biblical truths we have covered summon us to press on.

CHAPTER 3

A Biblical Anthropology and the Emotions

An anthropology class in college can be a real yawner. I enter this chapter with a plea: hang in through the theological part. It is important. It is, to misuse a phrase, "the missing link." It is only natural that we would go from considering God and his emotions to man, since man is made in the image of God. What the Bible says about us and who and what we are is not only the most important source of such information, but it is the sole authoritative source of information. All that the History Channel, the Discovery Channel, and The Learning Channel have to say, apart from the presuppositions of biblical revelation, is "knowledge falsely so called." Only a biblical theology of humanity can tell us what we are and who we are, as those created in the image and likeness of God. "In the most peculiar fashion, He chooses to reveal His perfect heart by analogy with human emotion that is stained by depravity. If we are to comprehend more richly the heart of God, it is imperative that we seek to understand our internal world."[1]

The history of man from the biblical standpoint is set in four distinct eras: man in his pre-fall state, man in his fallen state, man in his regenerate state, and man in his future state. Notice, the typical *Natural Geographic* stages are purposely missing.

Man in His Pre-fall State

In the very first chapter of the Bible we see God's creative power. The culmination of God's work of creation, the crown of his creation, is man. Here is how Moses put it:

> Then God said, "Let us make man in our image, after our likeness. And let them have dominion over the fish of the sea and over the birds of the heavens and over the livestock and over all the earth and over every creeping thing that creeps on the earth." So God created man in his own image, in the image of God he created him; male and female he created them. And God blessed them. And God said to them, "Be fruitful and multiply and fill the earth and subdue it and have dominion over the fish of the sea and over the birds of the heavens and over every living thing that moves on the earth." (Gen. 1:26–28)

God makes man, as male and female, in his own image and likeness. Although there have been a multitude of works on the meaning of the image of God, it seems that there are two complementary aspects. Think in terms of *what it does* and *what it is*.

The first element to the image of God is functional—what it does. This aspect of the image of God jumps out in the context. Man is made in the image and likeness of God and then is to *image* God by exercising dominion, being fruitful and filling the earth with other image bearers. The functional aspect of the image of God then emphasizes that man is to image or reflect God throughout the world through his God-given roles and responsibilities. God's intention is to fill the earth with his glory through human beings, made in his image, who are little glory reflectors.

Another aspect of the image of God is also clear. Man not only functions to image God, but he *is* the image of God. Man is in his person the image of God (the *what it is*). We see this most clearly not only in the words *image* and *likeness* but also in the next chapter where God breathes into man the breath of life, and man becomes a living soul (Gen. 2:7). Man's attributes, his characteristics, in the original creation are a reflection of the image of God in him.

Both of these aspects (what man is and what man does, i.e., the ontological and the functional), require that man must be an emotional being. He possesses emotions because he *is* the image of God. He is called to express emotions because he is called to *image* God. Our emotions exist because we are made in the image of God who has emotions. This is a vital ingredient to biblical anthropology. It is foundational as we approach our emotional life.

It seems safe to assume that before the fall all of Adam and Eve's faculties (mind, will, and emotions) worked in perfect harmony with each other. In their original creation, Adam and Eve had minds that accurately perceived truth and reality. They had emotions that properly responded to truth and reality. They had wills that in turn were properly motivated by unflawed emotions. Solomon seems to support this pre-fall alignment, writing, "See, this alone I found, that God made man upright" (Eccl. 7:29). Thomas Boston sums up man in his pre-fall condition:

> Man's understanding was a lamp of light. . . . His will in all things was agreeable with the will of God. . . . His affections were orderly, pure and holy; which is a necessary part of that uprightness wherein man was created. . . . Man's affections, then, in his primitive state, were pure from all defilement, free from all disorder and distemper, because in all their motions they were duly subjected to his clear reason, and his holy will.[2]

Their relationship with God and with each other would have reflected the harmony and purity of their understanding, their will, and their affections.[3]

Man in His Fallen State

We do not know how long man lived in this state. Needless to say, only two human beings (apart from the Lord Jesus) had ever experienced such internal harmony. When Adam and Eve fell, they plunged all their posterity into sin and death (Rom. 5:12). The fall of humanity affected every human being both legally and personally. In Pastor Albert Martin's words, in Adam we received "a bad record and a bad heart." Adam's sin was legally charged to all he represented (i.e., the entire human race), so that his legal guilt became our legal guilt. Adam's sin not only had legal implications, but it also had personal implications. Every human being who comes into this world has a nature polluted by sin. The infectious disease of Adam's sin has made its way into the bloodstream of his children. Every part of us, as human beings, has been infected by sin. This is the meaning of the term *total depravity*.

The Bible teaches that our minds have been polluted by sin. Romans 1:21, 28; 8:6–7 and Ephesians 4:17–18 all speak to the reality that in this fallen state our minds are filled with foolish speculations. This is not a reference to silly thoughts; it is a reference to an anti-God stream of consciousness. Our understanding has been darkened. Instead of the light of truth shining brightly in our minds, our minds are dark, filled with sin, and depraved and are unwilling and unable to submit to God and his revelation. This is not to say that we cannot think true thoughts or understand certain things about the world around us. It is not even to claim that we think only bad or evil things. It is to say however, that in our fallen state, we do not acknowledge God in our thinking, we do not submit our minds to his authority, and therefore we suffer from intellectual autonomy and mental impurity. The charge of corrupt and depraved minds cannot be honestly challenged. There is an annoying little prosecutor, called "conscience," who uses our daily experiences to convict us.

The Bible also teaches that our wills have been infected by sin. Although the debate over "free will" is a long-standing and complex debate, there is no lack of biblical evidence demonstrating that our wills—that part of our humanity that chooses—are also contaminated by sin. Our Lord Jesus says, "Truly, truly, I say to you, everyone who commits sin is a slave to sin" (John 8:34). No matter what some may say about free will, slavery is slavery. Fallen human beings are slaves to sin. This slavery includes our wills. Paul's testimony is equally devastating: "Do you not know that if you present yourselves to anyone as obedient slaves, you are slaves of the one whom you obey, either of sin, which leads to death, or of obedience, which leads to righteousness?" (Rom. 6:16). So why do we choose what we choose? Our "chooser" is in the straightjacket of our own fallen desires.[4]

Once during a prison Bible study in the drug and alcohol unit, I was teaching on the bondage of the will. One of the inmates bristled and then blurted out, "Preacher, do you mean to tell me that I don't have free will?"

"Yes, that is what I am saying the Bible teaches."

"I don't buy it!" he said irritably.

So I asked him, "Are you incarcerated for a drug- or alcohol-related offense?" The question was a safe one considering my location.

"Yes," he sheepishly replied.

I asked, "Have you ever wanted to stop abusing drugs and alcohol?"

A little humbled, he said quietly, "Yes. I've tried many times."

"If your will is free and you can do what you will, then why not just stop? The reason you can't just say 'no,' is that you are a slave. Your will is a slave to your own sinful nature."

End of debate, though, thankfully, not the end of the story.

This brings us to the sad fact that the Bible also teaches that our emotions have been infected by sin. Get the big picture: we have been corrupted by sin through and through. Our minds are fallen and corrupt. Our wills are in bondage to our depravity. And our emotions are defiled and disfigured by sin. Listen to God's indictment against us: "For my people have committed two evils: they have forsaken me, the fountain of living waters, and hewed out cisterns for themselves, broken cisterns that can hold no water" (Jer. 2:13). There is an insane emotional reversal that has taken place. That which is ultimately lovely and glorious and satisfying, namely God, has been forsaken by us because we love that which is unsatisfying and unlovely, namely sin. This is the heart of depraved emotions.

Again, the prophetic indictment comes thundering from the divine bench: "The heart is deceitful above all things, and desperately sick; who can understand it?" (Jer. 17:9). The heart, the seat of our innermost being, including the emotions, is sick and deceitful, so that we cannot even understand ourselves. There is an insane love for darkness rather than for light (John 3:19). It is not only a matter of *Why do I do the things I do?* but also of *Why do I love the things I should hate and hate the things I should love?* Why do I enjoy the moldy Vienna sausages of sin yet I am repulsed by the most succulent cuts of perfectly prepared filet mignon of Divine joys? Thomas Boston captures this radical depravity of our emotions with unforgettable language:

> The natural man's affections are wretchedly misplaced; he is a spiritual monster. His heart is where his feet should be, fixed on the earth; his heels are lifted up against heaven, which his heart should be set on. His face is towards hell, his back towards heaven; and therefore God calls him to turn. He loves what he should hate and hates what he should love; joys in what he ought to mourn for, and mourns for what he should rejoice in; glories in his shame, and is ashamed of his glory; abhors what he should desire, and desires what he should abhor.[5]

Like a Picasso painting, all our parts are distorted, out of place, backwards, and usually dark. The biblical portrait of us in our fallen state is unflattering. So much for self-esteem. The proper relationship of the emotions to the will and to the mind is twisted; it is out of order and out of proportion. We resemble a circuit board that at one time functioned properly and reliably, with all the components perfectly integrated. But since the fall, instead of our charges following the right paths, they deviate because of sin and cause serious malfunctions.

In other words, we short-circuit emotionally, mentally, and volitionally. Behavior, thoughts, and attitudes can trigger our emotions, but those behaviors, thoughts, and attitudes can be sinful, creating some serious malfunctions. Our emotions can also overpower or overcharge our thoughts, behaviors, and attitudes, blowing our fuses. The sad reality is that we are serious train wrecks!

Our emotions can be downright toxic. They can put such a stranglehold on our whole psyche that our fuse box is blown by their misdirected power surges. The effects are far-reaching. For instance, the Bible depicts many times the impact the emotions can have over the body. When David sinned, the impact of his guilt, along with all the emotional freight, pummeled him physically. "For when I kept silent, my bones wasted away through my groaning all day long. For day and night your hand was heavy upon me; my strength was dried up as by the heat of summer" (Ps. 32:3–4). The emotional wreckage of David's guilt had true psychosomatic effects. Psalm 38 and Proverbs 14:30; 17:22 reinforce the truth that the medical world is very aware of: the emotions are so powerful that they can affect the body and physical health.

The manifestations of fallen emotions are nearly limitless.[6] However, like many things in the Bible, not every emotion is either black or white. We need to qualify that not all emotional manifestations are sinful any more than all mental thoughts or volitional acts are sinful. There are also issues of physiology, personality, and temperament that may not be inherently sinful. Some of the following emotions are always sinful, while others may be appropriate at certain times under certain circumstances. With those caveats, consider that anger, hatred, bitterness, resentment, fear, anxiety, and worry can all be sinful emotions and sinful emotional expressions. Being easily offended, being driven by emotional impulses, and allowing the emotions to determine what is believed or what course of action is taken are reflections of sinful emotional states. Being unsympathetic, cold, indifferent, and as detached as the guards at Buckingham Palace is emotional malfunction and depravity. Allowing our emotions to cloud reality, to restrict what we believe or determine how we respond to truth, are other forms of emotional corruption.

To sum it up: our emotions have received the fatal infection of original sin and a fallen human nature. The toxicity of sin has permeated our emotions. Our emotions can short-circuit our whole system. The system is already broken. But the emotional power-surges or insufficient emotional power currents (the equivalent of an emotional brown-out) can further damage an already malfunctioning system. Man in his fallen state is pervasively ruined by sin in his mind, his will, and his emotions. Only redemption in Jesus Christ can begin the restoration project, rebuilding the ruins caused by sin. This reconstructive project begins with the new birth and is carried forward in sanctification.

Man in His Regenerate State

When God begins that wonderful work of redemption, it is a work on the whole person. Any view of saving grace that does not encompass the totality of our humanity is deficient. When the Spirit, the Lord and Giver of life, commences the work in time and space, he regenerates the sinner, and the sinner is converted. The act of regeneration is a sovereign act of the Spirit, which empowers once-dead sinners to turn from their sin and embrace the Savior. It is a glorious work.

In the process of this work the mind, the will, and the emotions all play an important role. We cannot assume that the Spirit works in the mind, the will, and the emotions with the same measuring stick. We also must not assume that the Spirit works in every new birth in exactly the same way.

For some, the supernatural work of the Spirit on the mind, enlightening them to the truth, is in the forefront. For others, their experience is of the Spirit hammering away at a stubborn will until he finally wins. For others still, their emotions play a very significant role. We dare not think that unless the Spirit pours out so much conviction, or gives this level of understanding or that degree of emotion that a person is not converted. But we also dare not think that regeneration and conversion leave certain parts of our humanity untouched. To one degree or another, conversion impacts the emotions, as well as the mind and the will. "True faith, in other words, inevitably gives rise to godly desires and emotions. . . . Regeneration always manifests itself in godly desires and emotions."[7]

Every person who enters the kingdom experiences some degree of being "poor in spirit" (Matt. 5:3). This is not merely cognitively coming to grips with our spiritual bankruptcy. It is more. It is being awakened to the reality of our destitute and undone condition (Isa. 6:5; John 16:8). There is an emotional element in realizing we are "poor in spirit," undone before a holy God, convicted by the Holy Spirit of our sins. Again, it will differ in *degree* from conversion to conversion, but it will not differ in *kind*.

Once peace with God comes through faith in Jesus Christ (Rom. 5:1), there is a joy that is an indispensable part of faith (Matt. 13:44; 1 Pet. 1:8). Not all Christians remember the day of their conversion, especially if they have been raised in a Christian home. But with true faith comes a level of joy, peace, satisfaction, and love. The Lord Jesus is precious, the truth of the gospel is satisfying, the forgiveness of our sins brings gratitude, and reconciliation with the

Father brings not only legal but also experiential peace. With new eyes and a new heart, the believer sees Christ as beautiful and as the all-satisfying Savior (John 6:35, 68). In regeneration and conversion the emotions have been touched, they have been reclaimed, and now the urban renewal project of the soul begins.

What happens in the redemptive process? Is God now committed to our nonstop enjoyment and prosperity? Is he governing and ordering the universe for our life, liberty, and pursuit of happiness? Thankfully, something much bigger and better than that is going on. I purposely have used words like *reclamation, renewal, restoration,* and *reconstruction.* In the redemptive process God begins to restore us to his image. It is a re-creation into the image of the One who is the perfect image of the Father, that is Jesus Christ (Col. 3:10; Rom. 8:29; Eph. 4:24).

Remember earlier we said that because we are made in the image of God we have emotions and are to express emotions? The fall ruined our emotional state because it ruined our state altogether. In redemption, God is putting things back into alignment; he is re-creating us in the image of Christ. This process of re-creation again entails every part of our humanity, so that our minds are being renewed (Rom. 12:2; Eph. 4:23; Col. 3:1–2), our wills are being brought into conformity with God's will (Mark 3:35; Phil. 2:12–13; 1 John 2:17), and our emotions are also being reconstructed, renewed, and realigned (1 John 2:15–17; Eph. 5:1–2). Love put in our hearts from God through the Holy Spirit (Rom. 5:5) is the seedbed for a whole garden of new affections.

Consider the nature of the kingdom we have entered. It is righteousness, peace, and joy in the Holy Spirit (Rom. 14:17). Consider the work of the Spirit as he bears his fruit in our lives (Gal. 5:22). Consider what now grieves us (Rom. 7:15). Are not these regenerate characteristics, and many more, nothing less than God changing our hearts and realigning our emotions as he progressively works in us? I realize that this point needs far more explanation and even defense. As we have seen and will see, some teach that we can do nothing about the emotions. I firmly believe such a view is unbiblical. It is also very harmful because it hinders our Christian growth and development in a very important part of our humanity. It also depreciates the fullness of the work of grace in our lives.[8]

Man in the Future State

When we are glorified (the consummation of our redemption), everything will finally be as it should be. As the line in the old hymn says,

> *Then we shall be where we would be,*
> *then we shall be what we should be;*
> *Things that are not now, nor could be, soon shall be our own.*[9]

Just as Adam and Eve in paradise had that perfect alignment of their human faculties, so we too, will, having experienced the completion of redemption, finally be all we were ever meant to be (Rom. 8:17–23, 28–29). One of the many thrilling prospects about the eternal state of the redeemed is the eternal increase of joy. In eternity we will be perfected in love, and we will perfectly enjoy that love (1 Cor. 13:8–13). When we reach the perfect state, we will be in the immediate, face-to-face presence of God, who is love. Jonathan Edwards speaks of this love and our experience of it:

> There, in heaven, this infinite fountain of love—this eternal Three in One—is set open without any obstacle to hinder access to it, as it flows forever. There this glorious God is manifested, and shines forth, in full glory, in beams of love. And there this glorious fountain ever flows forth in streams, yea, in rivers of love and delight, and these rivers swell, as it were, to an ocean of love, in which the souls of the ransomed may bathe with the sweetest enjoyment, and their hearts, as it were, be deluged with love! . . .
>
> And there, above all, we shall enjoy and dwell with God the Father, whom we have loved with all our hearts on earth; and with Jesus Christ, our beloved Savior, who has always been to us the chief among ten thousands, and altogether; and with the Holy Ghost, our Sanctifier, and Guide, and Comforter; and shall be filled with the fullness of the Godhead for ever![10]

At the beatific vision (seeing God face-to-face), we will become wholly perfected in the Trinity's love. We will participate in the unmitigated, untainted fullness of love that exists between the Father, Son, and Holy Spirit. We will love God in ways we have never known. We will experience God's love for us in ways we have never known. We will love each other in ways we have never known. There will not be one single heart that is not overflowing with the love of God; there will not be one dark corner of anger, bitterness, jealousy, or hatred. God's love will be all in all. Our perfected emotions will be beautifully responding to the realities of seeing our Savior, living in the new heavens and new earth, inhabiting glorified bodies, and being free from sin. This holy emotion of joy will only increase throughout eternity.[11]

In the meantime we cry out, "Come quickly, Lord Jesus!" In the meantime we search the Scriptures to understand better our emotions, asking God to give us the grace to conform those emotions to his holy Word and the image of our Lord Jesus Christ. What would our churches and homes look like if we were able to sanctify our emotions in greater measure? What kind of transformations would we see in our marriages and relationships if we experienced a biblical realignment of our emotions? Does the Bible offer such challenges and hold out such hope? I believe it does.

Part 2

Biblical Sanctification
and Our Emotions

CHAPTER 4

Our Emotions and the Authority of God's Word

Earlier I quoted an evangelical Bible teacher who said, "As a saved person, you can control your mind and your will, but not your feelings. God's plan is for us to *believe* Him and choose to submit ourselves to His loving care and authority regardless of how we feel. All together now, *Rain on how I feel!*"[1] It is common to hear such sentiments expressed one way or another about the emotions. The assumption often is, "They cannot be changed or governed; therefore, God cannot tell us how we should feel." Amazingly, even the useful *Self-Confrontation Manual* states, "*Note: God's Word never commands you to change your feelings, but you are commanded to change your deeds (thoughts, words, and actions) by being obedient to Scripture.*"[2]

Others categorize the emotions under temperament, personality type, or ethnicity. Once categorized, the emotions are then explained as "high D," introverted, bubbly, a fluffy puppy, choleric, Dutch, Irish, Italian, *ad infinitum*. Once we categorize certain emotional behaviors, we have put them into a special protective vault. The categorization effectively puts the emotions beyond the reach of sanctification and the biblical imperatives that would require change. I am not denying certain personality characteristics, but no classification of certain emotions and behaviors makes them exempt from the authority of God's Word. Martyn Lloyd-Jones's comments are worth quoting in full at this point:

> I have already been at pains to emphasize that all our temperaments are different, and I want to emphasize it again. But at this point I would say that although our temperaments are different, our temperaments should not make any difference at all face to face with the task. Now

61

here is the miracle of redemption. We are given our temperaments by God. Again, all our temperaments are different and that also is of God. Yes, but is must never be true of us as Christians that we are controlled by our temperaments. We must be controlled by the Holy Ghost. You must put them in order. Here are the powers and capacities and here is your particular temperament that uses them, but the vital point is that as a Christian you should be controlled by the Holy Spirit. What is so tragically wrong in a Christian is that he should allow himself to be controlled by his temperament. The natural man is always controlled by his temperament, he cannot help himself; but the difference that regeneration makes is that there is now a higher control even over our temperament. The moment the Holy Spirit enters in, He controls everything including temperament, and so He enables you to function in your own particular way through your temperament. That is the miracle of redemption. Temperament remains, but temperament no longer controls. The Holy Spirit is in control.[3]

God Cares about and Commands How We Feel

A careful reader of the Bible will conclude as indefensible any view that says, "The emotions are off-limits." Unless we are going to become lexical reconstructionists and change the semantic ranges and meanings of words, we must acknowledge that just as God authoritatively commands our moral decisions, he also authoritatively commands our emotions. God tells us how and what we should and should not feel. Our emotions are a part of our humanity that needs to be sanctified and brought under the authority of God's Word and into conformity with God's Word.

The redemptive process is for the whole person; the emotions are an inherent part of what it means to be a person. There are sinful emotional expressions that need to be repented of and put to death. There are Christlike emotions that need to be brought to life and cultivated. As we grow in grace, our emotions will increasingly reflect our new biblical values and evaluations. As godly emotions are cultivated, they will exert a powerful influence on our motives and our conduct.

John Piper has accurately pointed out that the Bible commands all kinds of emotions.[4] There is the divine imperative to be joyful or to rejoice (Matt. 5:12; Ps. 110:2; Rom. 12:8, 12, 15; Phil. 4:4). There is the command to "forgive your brother from the heart" (Matt. 18:35). Anyone who has dealt with forgiveness (who hasn't?) often says something to this effect: "I don't feel like I can forgive him yet." Forgiveness is more than an emotion, but whether we like it or not, it has an emotional element to it. We are also commanded to love. But "love is not a feeling," say a few Christian pop songs and teachers. This will not do. We are told to "love one another earnestly from a pure heart" (1 Pet. 1:22) and to "love one another with brotherly affection" (Rom. 12:10). Love may be more than a feeling, but never less.

There are also commands to fear (Luke 12:5; Rom. 11:20; 1 Pet. 1:17). Again, biblical fear, especially the fear of the Lord, has emotional elements to it. Biblical fear certainly is a response to biblical thinking, but it is thinking that moves the heart, stirs the emotions, and moves to action. There is the command to let the peace of Christ rule in our hearts (Col. 3:15). This peace is more than cognitive awareness; it is a feeling of rest and contentment. There is the command to be zealous: "Do not be slothful in zeal, be fervent in spirit" (Rom. 12:11). The idea is "to boil, to burn earnestly with devotion." "Well, that's not my personality" does not really seem like a good reason to disobey God's Word.

We are also told we need to desire the Word (1 Pet. 2:2). The analogy for this desire is the newborn babe who wants his mother's milk. There is nothing indifferent, dispassionate, or stoic about a hungry baby who longs for his mother's milk! The earnest, emotional appeals for milk in the dead of night can often wake not only those in the house but sometimes the rest of the neighborhood.

Tenderheartedness is also commanded (Eph. 4:32). How can a person be tenderhearted without engaging the emotions? As I write this section, I am recovering from a serious back surgery. I have been on my back for almost six weeks and have another four to go. People who know me know that this is killing me. I can't go for my daily run, I can't play ball with my sons, and my deer hunt is in jeopardy. Most importantly, I can't get to church and fellowship with people I love, and I can't preach.

As a result, those in the church have been coming to me. When they enter the house, they see their pastor lying on the hideaway bed, with his head shaved to prevent perpetual bed-head, skinnier than the last time they saw him, with the overall appearance of weakness. At such a sight, their hearts go out to me. I can see it on their faces. There is a tenderheartedness; they are moved emotionally, and I in return. They genuinely display feelings of tenderheartedness. Indeed, God commands us to be tenderhearted.

What about the commands to mourn? "Be wretched and mourn and weep. Let your laughter be turned to mourning and your joy to gloom" (James 4:9). What about the command to weep? "Weep with those who weep" (Rom. 12:15). Unless we want to resurrect the professional mourner of Jesus' day and fulfill these commands hypocritically, we are confronted with the command to cry real tears and authentically have broken hearts, which feel with others. These commands take place within certain contexts, under certain situations, and in light of certain truths, but do not miss the weight of these commands and others like them (Joel 2:17). God commands us to mourn, which engages the emotions. He commands us to weep, which expresses emotion.

There is another angle to this. Not only does God command certain emotions, but he also commands that we exercise self-control. Self-control is about as popular as root canals. Even among Christians, we seem to be enamored with how to have the best of what we want now. However, there is a serious requirement for believers to exercise self-control. It is a fruit of the Spirit (Gal. 5:23) and a gift of grace. "For God gave us a spirit not of fear but of power and love and self-control" (2 Tim. 1:7). God straightforwardly expects us to exercise self-control (Acts 24:25; 1 Cor. 9:25; 2 Pet. 1:6).

What is it about self that we are to control? We must control every aspect of our lives, especially our emotions. As Spirit-filled believers, we are to be in control of our emotions. We are to be sober-minded, reasonable, sensible, exercising good judgment and prudence (Rom. 12:3; 1 Pet. 4:7; 2 Tim. 2:12). The presumption is that our emotions are under the control of God's Word and Spirit and sound mental judgment.

The Bible authoritatively commands us to have and display certain emotions and to be in control of our emotions through Spirit-empowered self-control. To many this sounds impossible. "He might as well tell me to climb up on my roof, jump off, and fly!" If we are Christians, we *can* put off sinful emotions and we *can* cultivate godly emotions, no matter what our temperament, our ethnicity, or our personal history. Now here is the $64,000 question: "How do we obey these commands?" The fact that God commands is one thing. How to obey the command is something else.

Let me quickly say that there is no secret key, no prepackaged formula, and no seven easy steps. There is nothing easy in what I am about to say. But where there is a desire to change for God's glory, and where there is truth relevant to the desired change, we are in the position to change. We can begin to understand the truth, reject faulty thinking, and learn practical biblical application. Under the Holy Spirit's power, we can begin to develop new, godly habits while putting to death the old, ungodly ones. When we stop believing the lies of the Devil—that certain aspects of our life will never change—when Scripture begins to infuse us with the hope, and when we start practicing the truth we believe, there is change. Under the influence of the Word and Spirit, we really can begin to handle our emotions.

I wish there was a little pill we could take once a day for thirty days so that, at the end of the thirty days, we would be emotionally balanced people who had all of our ungodly, ugly emotions dead and buried and all the healthy, Christlike emotions thriving and glorifying God. Unfortunately, God has not ordained change in such a way. There are three significant pillars that we need to clearly erect and understand before we get to the nitty-gritty issues of mortification and cultivation. Those three pillars are (1) the foundation and priority of truth, (2) a sound theology of Christian experience, and (3) biblical examples of how to handle the emotions through truth.

CHAPTER 5

The Foundation and Priority of Truth

Truth always comes first. As Christians, we are dogmatically committed to "true truth." The sufficient and inerrant Word of God is the sum and substance of that truth. All of the truths we will be exploring are biblical truths that come straight from the pages of God's holy Word. The Word equals truth, truth equals the Word (John 17:17). The truth is of first importance when it comes to the gospel. The truth also comes first as we work out the gospel in the Christian life. We have been born again by the truth (James 1:18; 1 Pet. 1:23) and now are trying to live by the truth (James 1:22). This means that sanctification, increased conformity to the will of God, begins with and is shaped by the Word of truth (Rom. 6:17).

When we become Christians we gain a supernatural understanding of the truth (2 Cor. 4:6). Our enlightened minds, as new creations, have a new mental paradigm, giving us a new way of thinking. This new way of thinking is not "positive self-talk" based on "self-help." It is a new way of thinking based on our new understanding of truth. We have new eyes. So as we explore how to obey God's commands that involve the emotions and how to sanctify the emotions, we do not begin with the emotions or an emotional experience; we begin with the mind and the truth. Martyn Lloyd-Jones explains the process:

> Truth comes to the mind and to the understanding enlightened by
> the Holy Spirit. Then having seen the truth the Christian loves it. It
> moves his heart. If you see the truth about yourself as a slave of sin you
> will hate yourself. Then as you see the glorious truth about the love

of Christ you will want it, you will desire it. So the heart is engaged. Truly to see the truth means that you are moved by it and that you love it. You cannot help it. If you see truth clearly, you must feel it. Then that in turn leads to this, that your greatest desire will be to practice it and love it.[1]

Any attempt to sanctify the emotions, detoxify ourselves of hazardous emotions, and cultivate godly emotions must be built on the firm foundation of Christian truth. Any other program or process will be like trying to erect a skyscraper on a chicken-coop foundation. It will collapse. In order to sanctify the emotions we must have our minds renewed with the Word, washed with the Word, and reconstructed by the Word. Wrong thinking will lead to wrong feeling. Misperceptions about God, the gospel, Christ, the accomplishment and application of redemption, the nature of Scripture, the Christian life, and faith will cause emotional short circuits that will threaten our well-being. We must grip and be gripped by the truth. *It must be noted that we are not talking about truth as an abstraction; we are talking about truth as it exists in the person of God.* To truly encounter the power of truth is to encounter God in his Son (John 8:31–32, 36). "Encounter with God will not only change our emotions; most importantly it has the potential to change our hearts."[2]

Proverbs 23:7 states the importance of right thinking: "For as he thinks within himself, so he is" (NASB). Pastoral and personal experience have constantly taught me there are certain truths the Christian must understand, marinate in, and fully embrace in order to have spiritual and emotional equilibrium. There are many truths, which we may not agree on, and they will not put us in the tank (e.g., end-times views, modes and subjects of baptism, the gifts of the Spirit). Although these truths and many more are important, they are not critical to our spiritual and emotional health. They are the minerals and vitamins to our spiritual growth. However, some truths are oxygen. We cannot breathe without them. We cannot live without breathing. These oxygen truths are the character of God, justification, and future glory.

Oxygen Truth #1: The Character of God

The character of God is the core. It is the *sine qua non*, the "without which nothing." If we do not have the truth of God's character firmly fixed as foundational to all our thinking, then all effort in trying to obey God and sanctify the emotions will amount to our chasing our tails, ending in frustration. We must know who God is. Bruce Ware states, "To know this God, and better to be known by him (Gal. 4:9a), is to enter into the security and confidence of a lifetime of trust in his never-failing arms."[3] The theological North Star by which we will navigate the rest of this book is this: the most important thing about any one of us is *what we know about God* and *that we know God*. The Scripture supports this truth:

> Thus says the LORD: "Let not the wise man boast in his wisdom, let not the mighty man boast in his might, let not the rich man boast in his riches, but let him who boasts boast in this, that he understands and knows me, that I am the LORD who practices steadfast love, justice, and righteousness in the earth. For in these things I delight, declares the LORD." (Jer. 9:23–24)

> "For I desire steadfast love and not sacrifice, the knowledge of God rather than burnt offerings." (Hos. 6:6)

I still vividly recall sitting on the lawn at Biola University reading A. W. Tozer's *The Knowledge of the Holy* and soaking in these life-changing words: "What comes into our minds when we think about God is the most important thing about us."[4]

Reading A.W. Pink a couple of years later, I had a similar jolt when I read this: "Soothing-syrup may serve for peevish children, but an iron tonic is better suited for adults, and we know of nothing which is more calculated to infuse spiritual vigor into our frames than a Scriptural apprehension of the full character of God."[5]

My nonnegotiable premise in a book about the emotions is that we all must be good, God-centered, biblical theologians. I can hear someone object and say, "Hey, I just wanted to learn to control my anger. I'm not interested in being a theologian." Well, here is the truth that R. C. Sproul has been driving home for years now:

everyone is a theologian! The question is, are we good ones or poor ones? Poor theologians, those with low, unbiblical, unworthy views of God, will never grow in their emotional life as they ought. Good theologians, those who have a biblically robust, God-intoxicated theology, marinated in the riches of God's glories, will find their capacity to sanctify the emotions expand in life-changing ways.

Another related premise is this: *knowing God—who he is, what he does, what he is like, and what he requires of us—is the foundation for life and faith, joy, obedience, love, and worship.* Knowing God is eternal life (John 17:3). When we come into the new covenant by the work of Christ and the Holy Spirit, we know God (Jer. 31:31–34; 24:7). That relational knowledge is in an infant stage, but it is a real relationship with real knowledge. The requirement is that we grow in that knowledge. As we grow in the knowledge of God, our faith also grows. Psalm 9:10 states, "And those who know your name put their trust in you, for you, O Lord, have not forsaken those who seek you." God's name is not his title or his proper name, but rather it is his character, what he is like. The water level of faith rises in proportion to our growth in knowing God. Pink underscores this truth: "The foundation of all true knowledge of God must be a clear mental apprehension of His perfections as revealed in Holy Scripture. An unknown God can neither be trusted, served, nor worshiped."[6]

Not only does faith grow in proportion to our knowledge of God, but active obedience also grows as our knowledge of God grows. "But the people who know their God shall stand firm and take action" (Dan. 11:32). "Obedience to God is always based on a corresponding provision from God. God's actions of provision in the *past* lead to trust and hope in Him for the *future*, which in turn brings about obedience in the *present*. . . . Only knowing God Himself as He is revealed in His Word can create the kind of hope in His promises that brings about obedience to His will."[7]

A biblical understanding of the sovereignty, faithfulness, love, and goodness of God not only bolsters our faith, but it gives us emotional equilibrium and joy, peace, and a whole host of other godly emotions that can sustain us. A biblical understanding of God helps us to see his goodness in trials. A biblical vision of who God is compels us to give him the benefit of the doubt in the mysteries and trust him in the darkness. Such a high view of our great God promotes God-honoring feelings and helps immunize us from toxic, faith-threatening emotions.

A few years ago a number of women in our church wanted to organize a women's theology study group. The elders of our church agreed this was a great idea. We cannot say, "Everyone is a theologian; we are either just good ones or bad ones," and then quench people's desires to be better theologians. The women sought the counsel of their pastors and settled on Wayne Grudem's *Systematic Theology*. For three years they studied theology. One of the women wrote to me after they finished their first semester of study. Here is an excerpt from her letter, which illustrates the point I am trying to make:

> Studying theology has brought me *incredible joy*. Knowing God better and spending more time in His presence and beholding His beauty and glory make me *happy and content* in a way I have not known before. . . . Studying systematic theology is gradually bringing together into one coherent whole all the strands of teaching and Bible reading of 30-plus years. Everything is making much more sense, both biblically and in life. Hearing *the doctrine of God* preached has made me *mentally and emotionally healthier. I rarely suffer from depression now like I used to. A deep joy in the Lord is mine.*[8]

Oxygen Truth #2: Justification

Another oxygen truth is *justification by faith alone*. When I originally preached this series, justification was not very controversial, at least among Protestants. It seemed safe. There were a few renegade Protestants here and there who were getting wobbly over what some call "the New Perspective on Paul (NPP)." How quickly times change! This is now a front-burner issue. I have no significant interest in the NPP. I am not going to spend any time refuting the new view or defending the old view.[9] My complaint is that most people do not even know what the old perspective on Paul is, and, ironically, it is the old perspective on Paul, which is the ground of all true liberty, freedom, and joy in the face of a holy God.

The Reformation recovered a glorious truth: a sinner is declared righteous by a holy God through faith alone in Christ alone. Faith is the instrument of justification. The work of Christ is the ground of justification. The work of Christ entails both the life that he lived and the death that he died. He lived a perfectly righteous life, impeccably faithful to the law of God and unswerving in his confidence in God (Rom. 5:19). He lived the life we could never live. We call this the active obedience of Christ.[10]

Christ's obedience was not mechanical, formal, or merely external; it was true obedience that came from his heart. He lived a life of wholehearted obedience that flowed from a perfect love for and delight in God. Jesus cherished doing the will of God. "My food is to do the will of him who sent me and to accomplish his work" (John 4:34). "I delight to do Your will, O my God; Your Law is within my heart" (Ps. 40:8, NASB).

With every trial, every temptation and phase of life, Jesus grew in obedience (Heb. 5:8–9).[11] His ultimate demonstration of "active obedience" began on the night he was betrayed and faced the horror of the cross. He had said earlier in his ministry, "For this reason the Father loves me, because I lay down my life that I may take it up again. No one takes it from me, but I lay it down of my own accord. I have authority to lay it down, and I have authority to take it up again. This charge I have received from my Father" (John 10:17–18).

On the night of his betrayal, he began his greatest act of voluntary obedience to the Father. "Not as I will, but as you will" was his final answer (see Matt. 26:39–44). *Christ's obedience in death was the climax of his obedience.* "Who, though he was in the form of God, did not count equality with God a thing to be grasped, but made himself nothing, taking the form of a servant, being born in the likeness of men. And being found in human form, he humbled himself by becoming obedient to the point of death, even death on a cross" (Phil. 2:6–8).

This leads us right into the next aspect of justification, our

Lord's death. Some theologians have called this his "passive obedience." In reality, all of Christ's life was both active and passive obedience, as many have pointed out.[12] But we will work with the traditional categories. In his passive obedience, he lay down his life in death. His death was a substitutionary death. It was in our place. It was a penal death, that is, he paid the penalty for our sins (Rom. 5:8; Gal. 3:13; 1 Pet. 3:18). It was a propitiatory death, that is, he absorbed the wrath of God, which we deserved (Rom. 3:25; Heb. 2:17; 1 John 2:2; 4:10).

As Jesus was on the cross he cried out, "My God, My God, why have you forsaken me?" He paid the penalty of death; he was the target of divine white-hot, holy wrath. He suffered our hell right there on the cross. Hymn writer Annie R. Cousin captures the awe and wonder:

Jehovah bade His sword awake; O Christ, it woke gainst Thee;
Thy blood the flaming blade must slake, Thy heart its sheath must be.
All for my sake, my peace to make: Now sleeps that sword for me.

Justification is the great exchange. God took his sinless Son and put all our transgressions, sin, and filth on him and in turn took Christ's perfect righteousness and put it over us (2 Cor. 5:21). He punished his Son as he should have punished us, according to our sins. All that was condemnable in us was condemned in him so that we are forever free from condemnation (Rom. 8:1). Now he treats us as his own righteous Son deserves to be treated. We are forgiven and accepted as perfectly righteous. We are justified, redeemed, reconciled, and adopted in God's family forever. We cannot add anything to the work of Christ. It is completely finished (John 19:21). It sounds almost blasphemously audacious, but the words of this theologian are gloriously true: "We have in Christ all the righteousness God can require. We are as righteous as Christ Himself. Indeed, we have God's own righteousness—we have kept the covenant as faithfully as God Himself."[13]

What does this have to do with the emotions? If you believe that your acceptance with God depends on your performance or your works, if you believe that God treats you according to your good or bad conduct; you will be the emotional equivalent of Slinky after a three-year-old has tangled it up. No matter how much Dad tries to straighten out the twisted metal coils, it is an irreparable mess. The other alternative to thinking God accepts us on the basis of our performance is to be a self-deceived hypocrite. Neither option is very appealing.

Nothing gives emotional stability, authentic joy, and unshakable satisfaction like resting in the doctrine of justification by faith alone in Christ alone. The rallying cry of the Reformation, "Christ for me!" will give you a boldness and a strength that will go a long way in fighting off depression, frustration, and a whole anthill of ungodly feelings that erupt from a works-righteousness theology. The doctrine of free justification is a rock of solid joys and lasting pleasures. It is liberty; it is freedom, blessed freedom. Rightly apprehended and fully embraced, it becomes both a geyser of joy and Gibraltar of stability.

Oxygen Truth #3: Future Glory

The next oxygen truth has to do with eschatology. But not eschatology such as we are used to thinking about eschatology. What I am talking about has nothing to do with pre-, post-, or a-mill, horns, temples, or timelines. The oxygen truth of future glory is not tied into any one system; it is tied into something much bigger and much more certain. It is truth that has emboldened martyrs and comforted the suffering and the dying. If we are to walk in conformity with the emotional commands, sanctifying the emotions, then we must be infused with the truth and confidence of future glory. It is the reliable instrument panel on our plane when we are flying through the fog and have vertigo (Rom. 8:24–25).

Our best life is not yet. The Christian life though, is full of blessings, joy, and happiness but is not always trouble-free. It seems that certain believers have been the ordained goalie for the devil's javelin team. As Christians, we need to maintain a future-oriented faith, which locks like a laser on our future inheritance. No matter what the best sellers have to say about the Christian life, it is our future, eternal inheritance that provides emotional ballast for the child of God (Rom. 8:18).

Job, in spite of the little revelation he possessed and his frequent misjudgments about what God was doing, was sustained by what he knew of future glory. What he knew of future glory preserved his present hope. No honest reading of the book of Job can set forth Job as the poster child for unwavering faith and confidence. But even in the midst of incredible pain, he never lost sight of this: "For I know that my Redeemer lives, and at the last he will stand upon the earth. And after my skin has been thus destroyed, yet in my flesh I shall see God, whom I shall see for myself, and my eyes shall behold, and not another. My heart faints within me!" (Job 19:25–27). That confidence of the future sustained his present confidence. "Though he slay me, I will hope in him" (Job 13:15). "Faith is the response to the character of God, while hope springs from the promises God has made."[14]

Paul knew the same truth and lived by future-oriented faith, based on a fuller revelation. The perspective provided him with spiritual and emotional ballast that withstood wave after wave of violent storm. Why didn't he capsize emotionally? Paul was not only the apostle to the Gentiles; he was also the apostle of suffering (Col. 1:24). He was locked and loaded with a confidence in the future. He knew that no matter what happened today or tomorrow, God had made certain promises about the future. He knew that in the end God and his people win, and they win big. He had the oxygen mask of truth pumping the life-giving air into his lungs, strengthening his faith and sustaining his heart.

> So we do not lose heart. Though our outer self is wasting away, our inner self is being renewed day by day. For this light momentary affliction is preparing for us an eternal weight of glory beyond all comparison, as we look not to the things that are seen but to the things that are unseen. For the things that are seen are transient, but the things that are unseen are eternal. (2 Cor. 4:16–18)

The future weight of glory is oxygen truth that must flow through our spiritual bloodstream or else our faith platelets will get dangerously low, our hope will become anemic, and we will have a diminished capacity to value truth and keep an eternal perspective. Once this happens we will find ourselves at the bottom of one dark pit, and such commands as "Rejoice in the Lord" will seem to mock us. "Consider it all joy" will appear cruel. "Fear the Lord" will be empty. "Forgive from the heart," "love from the heart," will go in the circular file because of the seemingly obvious impossibility.

The summary of these oxygen truths is simple: knowing God—who he is and what he is like, what he has accomplished for us in his Son, and what he has in store for us in the future—is necessary for progress in emotional sanctification. Those aspects of God are foundational truths. They are life and health. To lay hold of these truths, to own them, to make them a conscious part of our thinking, will help tone our spiritual and emotional muscles. To breathe in these oxygen truths will increase our spiritual stamina and emotional vigor. When our emotions are increasingly aligned with the truth of who God is, what he has done for us in Christ, and what awaits us in the future, we will find our motives and our conduct aligning with God's Word.

CHAPTER 6

A Sound Theology of Christian Experience

The theological grid through which we live out our Christian experience is another vital component to sanctification and our emotions. Our view of Christian experience must be built on a biblical framework, or we might find ourselves "kicking against the goads." The first principle of sound Christian experience is that truth precedes, governs, and interprets experience, not vice versa. Truth first, experience second. "You will know the truth, and the truth will set you free" (John 8:32). The truth rightly embraced and believed will give you an experience.

What are the vital ingredients to sound Christian experience? What does biblically healthy Christian experience look like? What happens when my experience does not match what I believe? What happens when I do not feel like feeling as I am supposed to feel? Should I actively seek an experience? These are all good questions. Let's take them up.

A Balance and Tension between the Now and the Not Yet

There are certain views of Christian experience that are not only erroneous but also definitely harmful. Any view that is unbalanced can cause some serious emotional difficulties. Christian models of experience that expect spiritual attainments in the present but that are only going to occur in the age to come can create disillusionment with God and even with the Christian faith. Other models set forth virtually no expectations and allow wide margins for "carnal Christianity." These perspectives may not only dangerously deceive some unconverted people into thinking they are saved but also leave some real Christians in a near comatose state, passively waiting for God to do something.[1]

A biblical view of Christian experience must have a realistic perspective on what theologians call "the already and the not yet." Such a perspective comprehends what has been accomplished, what is being accomplished, and what will be accomplished. This keeps us balanced, realistic, hopeful, and motivated.

Every Christian must hold onto the reality that although there has been a definitive break with the old life, and there is now a radical new relationship with sin called *definitive sanctification*, there is also an ongoing battle between the flesh and the spirit (Gal. 5:17; Rom. 7:14–25). If I were a spiritual physician, I would recommend to every patient, as a matter of preventative health, to read John Owen's *Sin and Temptation*, J. C. Ryle's *Holiness*, Jerry Bridges's *The Pursuit of Holiness*, and John Murray's articles on sanctification.[2] Understanding the tension in sanctification between the already and the not yet is so important. Coming to grips with our death to sin and the continued struggle to put sin to death can keep us sane and hopeful.

When Sorrows Like Sea Billows Roll

Other harmful views of Christian experience are those that expect the Christian life to be a pain-free zone. As Christians, we must not only expect hand-to-hand combat with sin, but we must also know there is no exemption from suffering in this life. Suffering is not indicative of a lack of faith. Pain is not the direct result of our sins and failures. Certainly all suffering and pain is ultimately rooted in sin, but the notion that my pain and suffering is a payback from God is unbiblical. That is the theology of Job's comforters. The experience of solid, mature Christians throughout the ages has been one of suffering. A theology of Christian experience that says only blessing, health, and prosperity are the lot of the faithful is a recipe for emotional disaster with deep accompanying damage to faith. Such teaching is void of the very gospel itself.

Through him we have also obtained access by faith into this grace in which we stand, and we rejoice in hope of the glory of God. More than that, we rejoice in our sufferings, knowing that suffering produces endurance, and endurance produces character, and character produces hope, and hope does not put us to shame, because God's love has been poured into our hearts through the Holy Spirit who has been given to us. (Rom 5:2–5)

Resist him, firm in your faith, knowing that the same kinds of suffering are being experienced by your brotherhood throughout the world. And after you have suffered a little while, the God of all grace, who has called you to his eternal glory in Christ, will himself restore, confirm, strengthen, and establish you. (1 Pet. 5:9–10)

For it has been granted to you that for the sake of Christ you should not only believe in him but also suffer for his sake. (Phil. 1:29)

Again, if I were a spiritual physician and could prescribe some preventative medicine I would recommend D. A. Carson's *How Long O Lord?* Jerry Bridges's *Trusting God*, Joni Eareckson Tada's *When God Weeps*, and Jim Andrews's *Polishing God's Monuments*.[3] These books, among many others that could be mentioned, deal realistically with the place of suffering in the believer's experience. If we expect that "every day with Jesus is sweeter than the day before" we will be in for some serious disappointments. If we expect that victory over sin will be one uninterrupted triumph after another, we will become disillusioned with God, his Word, ourselves, or all of the above. A sound theology of Christian experience makes room for the struggle of the war-faring pilgrim and the suffering of the wayfaring pilgrim.

What If I Don't Feel Like It?

The next question that arises when it comes to Christian experience is what to do when we do not *feel* like doing what we should do. Because I am a pastor, people often ask me, "Isn't it better for me to stay home if I don't *feel* like going to church than to go to church when my heart isn't in it? Won't that make me a hypocrite?" My answer is, "No, it will only make you a chain sinner, lighting up one sin with another." After a puzzled look, I explain.

If God commands us to do something and we don't do it, what

is our normal course of action? Confession and repentance. Why should the protocol be any different when we fail to feel the way God commands us to feel? If he commands us to come and worship him with gladness (Ps. 100:1–2), yet we don't feel like worshiping him with gladness, *that is a sin*.[4] If we have no joy at the prospect of gathering with God's people on his day to sing his praise there is some serious darkness in our hearts and some mixed-up priorities. The lack of joy is sin. Confess it. "Father forgive me for not taking joy in what ought to be the true joy of my heart." And then repent, bringing forth fruits in keeping with repentance by going to church. Even if your heart does not change right away, do what you are supposed to do with a repentant heart. What you will find is that the power comes in the doing. God will forgive us and our hearts will change in the process.

Should I Seek an Experience?

The next common question about Christian experience is "should I seek an experience with God?" Once upon a time, I was an experience junkie. I would go to this meeting or that service to hear this preacher or that evangelist, hoping for some experience. The sought-after experience was for the sake of the experience alone. Later in my Christian life I rejected that approach wholesale. Experience became anathema.

Then I discovered the Puritans and their heirs and realized that they thought much about Christian experience, but not in the same way I did. My eyes were opened to see that doctrine and experience were not enemies, or mutually exclusive. However, there is a priority in our seeking. We need to seek God, not an experience. We need to seek the truth and a greater knowledge of the Word, not experience. Many times, in God's sovereign grace, he may grant extraordinary spiritual experiences, but those are merely the reactions to encountering God in truth.

As we worship God, we ought to long to experience the presence of God through his Holy Spirit. But the worship must be in Spirit and truth (John 4:24), not just in scintillating music. Music moves us, but we must make sure that music is the vehicle for truth. Preaching can and should move us, but it must be through truth. Again, truth must be the priority, and experience will often follow.

The Bible authoritatively commands our emotions. God expects us to feel certain ways and to sanctify our emotions. In this process the Word of God has the priority. The emotions are transformed through truth and biblical thinking. There are certain truths essential for our life and emotional wholeness: the character of God, justification by faith, and future glory. The priority of truth in the transformation of the emotions also requires a sound theology of Christian experience. We cannot afford to misunderstand our struggle with sin or suffering. We cannot afford to live by emotional impulses; we must live by the truth. We cannot be experience seekers; we must seek God as he is revealed in his Word. These are the foundational perspectives necessary to move forward in spiritual and emotional growth. Now we will see biblical examples of how to handle the emotions through the truth of God's Word.

CHAPTER 7

How to Handle the Emotions through Truth

As we grow, we want to be more like our Father (Matt. 5:44) and more like the Lord Jesus (Phil. 2:5; 1 Pet. 2:21; 1 John 2:6). We want to be conformed to their image (Col. 3:10). Our being conformed is a reconstruction project. During the reconstruction, we are learning to direct our emotions to respond properly to the truth. We are learning to conform our emotions to the truth. We should view the emotions as good, although fallen, and a part of God's image in us and an inherent part of our humanity. The goodness of human emotions was perfectly modeled by our Lord Jesus.

But in order for our emotions to be sanctified and honoring to God, they must properly respond to truth, and we must handle them by truth, which is why I reiterate here that truth is always found in the person of God himself, and ultimately it is the encounter with God through truth that changes us. "The pathway to a life of obedience born of hope is ultimately *not something we follow but someone we encounter*."[1]

As redeemed people, we see how important the Word of God is to us. It is our infallible guide to our emotional life. The Word is the foundation upon which we build our emotional sanctification. "The way that we know what he wants us to desire and feel is by reading the Scriptures and noting what his saints are represented as properly desiring and feeling as well as what God commands and counsels his saints to desire and feel."[2] The Word through the Spirit helps us not to suppress our emotions but to cultivate and communicate them with Spirit-empowered self-discipline. The Word is also the kindling that stokes the fire of authentic Christian experience and godly emotions. We can observe this pattern in the Bible itself. In the following section we are going to explore a few examples in Scripture.

The Psalms

We begin with the Psalms. My former Hebrew professor Ron Allen used to say, "Only a Philistine could fail to love the Psalms."[3] We begin with the Psalms because the Psalms are poetry, and poetry is the language of experience. Poetry is designed to be felt. C. S. Lewis captures this: "Most emphatically the Psalms must be read as poems: as lyrics, with the licenses and all the formalities, the hyperboles, the emotional rather than logical connections, which are proper to lyrical poetry. They must be read as poems if they are to be understood."[4] In particular we will begin with the lament psalms because they are not the jubilant songs of praise; they were written from the depths. The lament psalms are concrete examples of how to handle the emotions through the truth. The typical components of a lament psalm usually are:

- an address, an introductory petition and lament;
- the lament proper;
- the confession of trust;
- the petition;
- the vow of praise.

There are many variations, but there is no mistaking these psalms. They have the common denominator of grief. There is disappointment, sadness, sorrow, sickness, depression, darkness, crying, distress, and complaint. These psalms capture the depth of human emotion in all of its rawness. The nerves are exposed; there are no pretexts, no pretensions, just pure pain. The distress in these psalms is not *necessarily* sinful. However, it is safe to say that if the psalmist had not dealt with his emotions in the manner expressed in the laments, he could have easily crossed over the sin-county line. Therefore, these psalms give us a biblical model for dealing with difficult times and tough emotional circumstances.

Psalm 6 begins with an avalanche of emotions. Fear, anxiety, inner pain, and outer pain all come tumbling in on the psalmist.

> *O* LORD, *rebuke me not in your anger,*
>> *nor discipline me in your wrath.*
> *Be gracious to me, O* LORD, *for I am languishing;*
>> *heal me, O* LORD, *for my bones are troubled.*
> *My soul also is greatly troubled.*
>> *But you, O* LORD—*how long?*
> *Turn, O* LORD, *deliver my life;*
>> *save me for the sake of your steadfast love.*
> *For in death there is no remembrance of you;*
>> *in Sheol who will give you praise? (Ps. 6:1–5)*

John Goldingay describes the psalmist's condition as "inner panic as well as outer trembling."[5]

Verse 6 "underlines the suppliant's distraught state."[6] "I am weary with my moaning; every night I flood my bed with tears; I drench my couch with my weeping." Verse 7 shows the physical effects of the distress: "My eye wastes away because of grief; it grows weak because of all my foes." Anyone who has suffered does not laugh or scoff at these words but resonates with them. They are hyperbole, but hyperbole to capture the depth of pain that goes beyond words. In the psalm there is also the added aggravation of those who are making the inner turmoil of the sufferer more insufferable. Insult is added to injury. But then there is a shift, "a sudden and radical change in atmosphere."[7]

> *Depart from me, all you workers of evil,*
>> *for the* LORD *has heard the sound of my weeping.*
> *The* LORD *has heard my plea;*
>> *the* LORD *accepts my prayer.*
> *All my enemies shall be ashamed and greatly troubled;*
>> *they shall turn back and be put to shame in a moment. (Ps. 6:8–10)*

The psalmist chases away with a statement of faith those who increase his affliction: "Yahweh has heard my weeping. Yahweh has heard my plea. He has accepted my prayer." Why is there such a change of emotional direction? Why is there is a new confidence?

It does not come from God *already* accomplishing something on behalf of the sufferer, but it comes because the sufferer is convinced of the truth that his God hears his prayers and *will* answer his prayers. He is rescued from the depths because he believes something true about God. Goldingay appropriately states, "The stance is *between* assurance that Yhwh is committed to action and experience of the action itself."[8] The truth that God hears his prayers and sees his pain pulls the psalmist out of the ocean of tears and fills him with confidence that God is faithful.

Psalm 16 puts this pattern in principle form: "I have set the LORD always before me; because he is at my right hand, I shall not be shaken. Therefore my heart is glad, and my whole being rejoices; my flesh also dwells secure" (Ps. 16:8–9). The psalmist, David, says that he has set Yahweh before him. David keeps the truth of who God is and what God is like in the forefront of his mind. He did not occasionally think about God; he regularly thought about God. David knew that what he thought about God was the most important thing about him.

David does not stop there. He goes on. Yahweh is at his right hand, the place of support, immediate presence, honor, and authority. David's support and strength is the presence and power of his God. The result of mentally keeping Yahweh before him and the result of having Yahweh as his constant power and presence is that David is not shaken. He is stable and strong. Truth about God and trust in God form immovable pillars. As if that weren't enough, David then says there are emotional results: gladness, rejoicing, and felt security. The truth of God coupled with trust in God's presence and power caused David to flourish emotionally with joy and security. "This provides the basis for a joyful confidence for the future that embraces the whole person."[9] Truth fueled and shaped the emotions.

The psalms reveal this pattern in a multitude of ways. Such psalms as 42–43 and 77, among many others, express the same patterns of disorientation, distress, and pain. In each occasion, what pulls the psalmist through is not the placebo of self-help talk, but God-centered truth. The Psalms expose the heart, lay bare the emotions, and point us to God, his Word, his promises, and his ways again and again. The heart is stabilized, and faith flourishes under such circumstances.

The Lamentations of Jeremiah

Another powerful example of how to handle the emotions through truth comes to us from another poetic portion of Scripture, the book of Lamentations. To the modern evangelical, Lamentations seems a little strange. When we get to chapter 3, it says some pretty harsh things about God. It is pure agony. Lamentations is open-wounded, inside-out misery. Jeremiah loved and ministered to a recalcitrant people who rejected him and his message. He poured himself out for the sake of his people and his God. No one listened. Instead, they gladly listened to the false prophets of nationalism and peace and prosperity. Finally, Jeremiah's prophecies were fulfilled and the Babylonian war machine came in with tsunami force.

Jerusalem lay in a heap of smoldering rubble. The stench of death permeated the air. The prophet's heart, which had already been broken time and again, is now ripped out of his chest, seemingly without mercy. In this brutal brokenness, Jeremiah picks up his pen. With tears and gut-wrenching grief, he writes. He writes from the heart. He writes theology. He writes poetry—yes, poetry. John Piper observes, "Lamentations is a deeply emotional book. Jeremiah writes about what means most to him, and he writes in agony. . . . If there was ever intensity and fervor in the expression of passion from the heart, this is it."[10]

In the midst of grief and true, honest-to-God complaints (3:1–18), Jeremiah reaches what looks like a desperate crescendo of someone whose faith is hanging by a thread: "Remember my affliction and my wanderings, the wormwood and the gall! My soul continually remembers it and is bowed down within me" (Lam. 3:19–20). "O God, please remember my pain! I can't forget it. It feels like someone has slugged me in my emotional solar plexus. I can't breathe. I can't stand up. O God, remember me." And then there is a breakthrough. Something happens. The winds of emotion shift, and they shift because Jeremiah begins to *think*. He begins to preach truth to himself. He begins to embrace truth, and the truth begins to do its work. Listen carefully to what he says:

> But this I call to mind,
>   and therefore I have hope:
>
> The steadfast love of the LORD never ceases;
>   his mercies never come to an end;
> they are new every morning;
>   great is your faithfulness.
> "The LORD is my portion," says my soul,
>   "therefore I will hope in him."
>
> The LORD is good to those who wait for him,
>   to the soul who seeks him. (Lam. 3:21–25)

Notice the first step, "This I call to mind." In the midst of an emotional vortex Jeremiah gets a grip by means of what he thinks. What does he think? Does he just let his mind go to a happy place far away? No. He starts thinking thoughts about God—who God is and what he is like. He starts to think true things about God. We can hear him preaching to himself something like this:

God's covenant love never ceases; that is a fact. It is what the instrument panel of the Word tells me even though I feel like I am upside down. His mercies never come to an end. That is a fact. Even though my sight tells me there is no mercy in God, his Word assures me otherwise. His mercies are new every morning. That is a fact. God never asks me to live on yesterday's mercy; he gives fresh mercy every day, no matter what the Devil says.

Great is his faithfulness. That is a fact. He is a rock of faithfulness; his track record is flawless. The history of his people and the history of my life are filled with monuments of unfailing faithfulness. This is what I know to be true about God. The circumstances of what I see cannot change these truths. When these truths grip my mind and I preach them to myself, something happens. The LORD is my portion. God reemerges as my treasure and my ultimate inheritance. Eternal perspective begins to blow away the fog of emotional confusion. Therefore, I will hope in him.

Truth triumphs over the feelings of despair. It ropes in the restless, uncontrolled feelings. Biblical equilibrium is restored, and hope, confident expectation, is restored. Another petal of truth blossoms: God is good. Right there in the middle of the death stench, truth triumphs over sight and regains control of the feelings, and the heart says, "God is good." The response to this truth, which entails right thinking, biblical volition, and faithful feelings, is "I can wait for him and seek him and bank my confidence on his goodness." Hallelujah! We can get a grip on the emotions through the truth and redirect them toward faith in God.

2 Corinthians 1:8–10: Paul's Lesson in Asia

There are many New Testament examples of a single truth and pattern. I want to focus on one of my favorites. I trust that as the truth is expounded and the pattern is revealed, your own eyes will be opened to see it repeatedly as you read your own Bible.

The apostle Paul knew affliction, tribulation, and trials with a firsthand experience that makes most of us soft Americans shudder. But there was one affliction that outweighed them all. Something happened to Paul in Asia that would forever mark him. The lessons are profound, and the Holy Spirit inspired Paul to reflect on them for our instruction.

In 2 Corinthians 1:8–10 Paul speaks of an affliction that came to him while he was in Asia. The description of the affliction is overwhelming: "For we were so *utterly* burdened *beyond* our strength that we despaired of life itself. Indeed, we felt that we had received the sentence of death" (vv. 8–9a). The severity of the affliction is captured by the word *burdened*, which implies a heaviness that is difficult to bear. Paul then qualifies the burden, the weight he bore, as going beyond any standard of measurement he could use. "If we had a burden graph, this was off the charts!" Putting it all together, he was burdened, weighed down beyond measure, and beyond his ability to bear it. "He knew that, humanly speaking, he was in over his head, both physically and emotionally."[11]

The conclusion is stunning. "We despaired of life itself." Better yet, "We *super*-despaired of life." There is despair and then there is super-despair. The sentence of death that hung over his head probably meant the affliction was so intense and the despair so severe that it seemed death was the only way out. As the great apostle surveyed the affliction and asked, "What are my prospects?" seemingly the sole voice that answered back said, "Only death, Paul, only death!"

Before we move on, we must ask, "What was Paul's affliction?" There have been many guesses. The most prominent is some severe illness. The fact is we do not know. What we do know about this particular affliction was that it stood out, head and shoulders above other afflictions in the lives of Paul and his companions, and it was so severe that he was weighed down; he despaired of life, and he saw death as the only prospect.

I want to make sure that we see and feel what Paul is saying. We can so super-spiritualize the Christian life that we do not leave room for the times of deep, painful, faith-shaking affliction. Paul knew the reality and power of Christ's strength: "I can do all things through him who strengthens me" (Phil. 4:13). He knew the reality of not reaching that place of utter despair: "We are afflicted in every way, but not crushed; perplexed, but not driven to despair" (2 Cor. 4:8). But here in the beginning of the letter he was recounting his experience of a place that was so dark and so deep that it was not just a matter of quoting a verse and pulling himself up by his Bible bootstraps.

From the deepest and darkest corner of this "my only way out is death" pit, Paul caught a glimmer of something. He saw something, or rather, was shown something. A truth gripped him and guided him out of the despair. Read his words aloud: "We had the sentence of death within ourselves so that we would not trust in ourselves, but in God who raises the dead; who delivered us from so great a peril of death, and will deliver us, He on whom we have set our hope. And He will yet deliver us" (2 Cor. 1:9b–10, NASB). The "so that" trumpets forth, "There is a purpose, a divine purpose, even in affliction and despair!" The depth and despair have a divine "so that," a lesson to learn, a truth by which to be changed.

The first truth is in the negative: ". . . so that we would not trust in ourselves." Here was the temptation: to trust self, to rely on self, and to have self-confidence, a sense of self-sufficiency. Someone says, "O not Paul!" O yes! Not even Paul was immunized from such temptations. This man had unparalleled experiences, the highest education, unsurpassed gifts, and an indomitable strength. Paul says, "God let me go so low and let it get so dark because he wanted to teach me not to trust myself, and he wanted to teach me something about him."

The second truth is positive: ". . . in God who raises the dead." God requires that his servants be those who put their confidence in him. Paul is sharing a truth about God. The God who powerfully raised Christ from the dead is the God who raises us out of our "death is my only prospect" death. The God we trust is the God of resurrection power and life.

Paul then celebrates the divine deliverance: "[He] delivered us from so great a peril of death." Murray Harris notes, "He apparently viewed his deliverance from the affliction as a veritable resurrection from the dead brought about by God, because he assumed that his death at that time was inevitable; he was as good as dead."[12]

Paul, armed with truth, now gains a restored confidence: "[He] will deliver us." The future tense indicates Paul knew that this affliction was not over; it could recur, but he had learned the divine lesson and embraced the divine purpose. He further expresses it, "He on whom we have set our hope." This truth—who God is, especially as a God of purpose and resurrection power—reinvigorated Paul's hope and confident expectation. The truth brought about an emotional one-eighty, from despairing of life to a renewed confidence in the God who raises the dead. That one-eighty catapulted Paul's rejuvenated faith forward. It was a lesson learned, a hope revived, and a reality reminded.

The truth about God, his sovereign purpose, and his resurrection power was an emotional lifeline that rescued Paul. Truth apprehended and truth applied realigned his emotional vertigo and brought him back to stability, faith, and confidence in God. God staged the events that led to the despair and then used the power of truth to buoy up his sinking apostle.

Psalmists, prophets, and apostles were all real people with real struggles. They were not given some special exemption from distress or some pass to live a pain-free life. "It is actually within the inner mayhem of life that a stage is built for the intrusive story of His light and hope."[13] Their lives are grand stages for lessons of God's light and hope. As these saints hit bottom, when their faith burned low, when their emotional tank's needle tottered on empty, they knew what to do. Do we know what to do? Let's learn from them. Fill your mind with truths about God. Embrace the truth and use it to gain emotional balance. In order for faith to triumph over sight, we need to fire up faith with the kindling of truth—who God is, what he is like, what he has promised for the future, what he has done in the past, and what he is for us in the present must flood our minds. We must take up our cotton cloths and begin polishing all of God's monuments of faithfulness with vigor.[14]

As the floodwaters of truth fill the heart and reminders of his faithfulness fill our memories, we find our faith rising higher and higher and our emotions stabilizing. But our emotions do more than merely stabilize. We can find our emotions responding to truth such that we are gladly trusting, truly rejoicing, and resting with a contentment of heart that surpasses any human explanation.

One of my dearest friends was the first deacon in our church. When I met him, his wife was dying of lymphoma. He clung to God's Word. When she went home to be with the Lord, he continued to cling to God's Word. God's promises of the future were precious to him. God's promise to sustain him was his anchor: "As your days, so shall your strength be" (Deut. 33:25). He reveled in reading about the character of God. For ten years he lived as a bachelor, content in the Lord with a steady and happy faith.

He remarried in the twilight of life. Everyone was happy for him and rejoiced with him and his new bride. But life quickly turned south; the marriage apparently was not made in heaven. After suffering for three years he was asked to leave his home. The situation was ugly and humanly hopeless. The humiliation would have been more than most men could bear, and yet he bore it with dignity and faith, really believing in the sovereignty of God and the goodness of God. Was he brokenhearted? Yes. But not crushed or bitter. He simply put his hope in the God who raises the dead and whose mercies are new every morning.

Shortly after the separation, he was diagnosed with leukemia. He never complained. What came out of his mouth was only that which was in his heart: "God is good and he does good. He is so much better to me than I deserve." He finally left the land of the dying and went home to be with Christ. The last few years of his life, which should have been the brightest, were the darkest. But his life was a stage for the light and hope of God to burn brightly. He clung to the Word, he banked his hope on God's character, and he died in faith. He is one of my heroes who reminds me that the truth of God sustains faith and gives us joyful contentment, even when our hearts are breaking.

Part 3

Mortifying
Ungodly Emotions

CHAPTER 8

An Introduction to Mortifying Ungodly Emotions

Mortification is an old word. When used today, it probably never means what the Authorized Version and the Puritans meant. Someone today might say, "When I saw her dip her New York steak in Ranch dressing I was *mortified!*" Far, far from the minds of moderns is this usage: "For if ye live after the flesh, ye shall die: but if ye through the Spirit do *mortify* the deeds of the body, ye shall live" (Rom. 8:13, KJV). That is the way the Puritans used the word. John Owen's classic work contains a section entitled, "The Mortification of Sin."

The word *mortify* or *mortification* used in the King James Version and by the Puritans was derived from the Latin word *moritificatio*, which was used to translate the Greek word *apothnēskō*, meaning "to put to death." When we talk about mortifying sin or mortifying ungodly emotions, we are simply talking about the sanctification process whereby we learn to put sins to death. This is the negative side of the Christian's duty. The positive side is to vivify (bring to life) or grow and cultivate certain Christian graces and godly emotions. In this very practical section, we are going to unfold the process of dealing with ungodly emotions that the Bible identifies as sin.

Honest Self-evaluation

There are three preliminary steps in attempting to put to death ungodly emotions. First, we must have some level of understanding of ourselves and our emotional makeup. The apostle Paul urges honest self-evaluation: "For by the grace given to me I say to everyone among you not to think of himself more highly than he ought to think, but to think with sober judgment, each according to the measure of faith that God has assigned" (Rom. 12:3).

I could personally fund foreign missions for a decade if I had a dollar for every time during a counseling session I have heard, "I don't have an anger problem"; "I am a pretty level-headed guy"; "I don't usually get stressed very easily"; and "Well, I have never been the jealous type." All the while I am hearing these statements, I am looking right into the face of someone who is wound tighter than a top, or who is about to blow a gasket. You get my point. Paul is telling us that we are not to have unrealistic views of ourselves. We should not elevate ourselves, thinking we are better than we are. We need to have a sober, honest, realistic evaluation of ourselves.

We need to identify honestly patterns of sinful emotions and emotional displays. We might need help doing that. We might find it difficult to locate someone who is willing to be brutally honest with us, because of our sinful emotions. But it must be done. Without getting defensive, we must make ourselves vulnerable to the truth of Proverbs 27:6: "Faithful are the wounds of a friend." We should pray that God would help us to search our hearts and help us to see where we are falling short (Ps. 139:23–24). We need to pray for an open ear and heart if we are to change (Prov. 10:17; 12:1, 15; 15:5, 10, 12, 31, 32; 19:20, 25, 27; 21:11).

Once we begin to identify the problem areas, we must isolate the patterns of our sinful emotions from all excuses and causes, both legitimate and imagined. To say, "I only get angry with my wife and nobody else," is blame-shifting, which is counterproductive and sinful. Remember, seeing sin in ourselves is not easy. We are fighting self-deceit (Jer. 17:9) and self-justification (Luke 10:25–29). Our first line of defense is to say we are not that bad or our situation is not really a problem.

Our second line of defense is to make excuses for why we act the way we do. "It's his (her) fault" or "we can't help it" (Jer. 18:11–12). All that this amounts to, no matter what the form, is fig-leaf theology, defense mechanisms that relieve us of personal responsibility. This is a time for ruthless honesty in identifying our sinful emotions, focusing only on ourselves as the culprits.

Martyn Lloyd-Jones makes this point: "We must start by knowing ourselves and by understanding ourselves. . . . Do we know ourselves? Do we know our particular danger?"[1] He does caution us about the differences between being introspective and being an extrovert. We need to know which way we are bent. The introspective person can take the call to know himself and turn it into an unhealthy rummaging through his own feelings, scraping and scratching his insides. The extrovert, on the other hand, takes a quick glance and moves on, never thinking seriously that he might have a major fault. We must follow the words of Paul with judgment-day honesty; we must evaluate ourselves with sober judgment.

Confession and Repentance

The second basic step, after we have identified the ungodly emotion such as bitterness, anger, or fear, is to be quick to own it and confess it to the Lord without excuse. Proverbs 28:13 teaches us, "Whoever conceals his transgressions will not prosper, but he who confesses and forsakes them will obtain mercy." The mercy comes when we own our sin, stop concealing it or excusing it, and take full responsibility for it. When we do that, the mercy pipe is unobstructed, and we are in a place to receive not only forgiveness (1 John 1:9) but also the grace to change.

This confession begins with God. We confess our sins to him (1 John 1:9). But we must also recognize there may be others around us who have been wounded and sinned against by our ungodly emotions. We must go to them, as well, in genuine confession, seeking their forgiveness, not merely telling them we are sorry (James 5:16). Confession to another person is critical. The Puritan Thomas Manton describes the process: "Confession is an act of mortification, it is as it were the vomit of the soul; it breeds a dislike of the sweetest morsels when they are cast up in loathsome ejections; sin is sweet in commission, but bitter in remembrance."[2] Dietrich Bonhoeffer demonstrates the breakthrough that confession brings:

Sin demands to have a man by himself. It withdraws him from the community. The more isolated a person is, the more destructive will be the power of the sin over him, and the more deeply he becomes involved in it, the more disastrous is his isolation. Sin wants to remain unknown. It shuns the light. In the darkness of the unexpressed it poisons the whole being of a person. This can happen even in the midst of a pious community. In confession the light of the Gospel breaks into the darkness and seclusion of the heart. The sin must be brought into the light. The unexpressed and hidden is made manifest. It is a hard struggle until sin is openly admitted. But God breaks gates of brass and bars of iron (Ps. 107:16). Since the confession of sin is made in the presence of a Christian brother, the last stronghold of self-justification is abandoned.[3]

True confession to our heavenly Father and true confession to others should flow from a fountain of real repentance. When we begin to see ungodly, sinful, toxic emotions in ourselves, we begin to see that they dishonor our Father and do harm to those around us, especially those closest to us. Confession is the first step in authentic repentance, and authentic repentance is determination to change for Christ's sake and with Christ's help.

So let's say that God helps me to see that I get angry when I don't get my way. When that anger is manifest, it comes out with mean words or with the silent treatment. So I confess it to the Lord. I confess it to those who have been on the receiving end. Then there is a resolve to put that sinful emotion to death. I must really want to put that sin to death for the right reasons before I will ever make genuine efforts to do it. What tools do we need to kill the monster of our ungodly emotions?

Thankfully, we do not need to search high and low for the silver bullet. God has given us everything we need (Eph. 1:3; 2 Pet. 1:3). After owning our sin and having a real desire to change, we need someone with whom we can be transparent and who will be honest with us. We need someone who will not hesitate to confront us in love. We need someone who will not condemn us when we tell them of failures or struggles.

Although some see the idea of accountability partners as nothing more than a trend, there is a place for the kind of friendships in which Hebrews 3:12–13 can happen. "Take care, brothers, lest there be in any of you an evil, unbelieving heart, leading you to fall away from the living God. But exhort one another every day, as long as it is called 'today,' that none of you may be hardened by the deceitfulness of sin." In chapter 19 we will spend more time on meaningful Christian gathering and fellowship. For now, we are focusing on our need for a person who will speak honestly and listen lovingly as we seek to put to death ungodly emotions. It is often at this very point where our commitment to real change is put to the test.

Learn the Biblical Process

The other set of tools we need in our box is an understanding and implementation of the repentance-mortification-transformation (i.e., the sanctification) process. The process in most cases is not hard or complex, but there is a commitment that is required to stay on track. It is far too easy to experience some conviction, pluck up the courage to talk about it with someone once or twice, do better for a week, and then drop it like a hot rock. The tools are readily available to us in Scripture, but it takes some work and determination.

The first tool is not a hammer; rather, it is special lenses that set things in perspective. In other words, we start with right, biblically oriented thinking about the sinful emotion. Many times we never wake up to the terribleness of our sin because we never look at it through the lenses of Scripture. Once seen through the lenses of our Bibles, we begin to see that our particular sins are not merely "peccadilloes"; we see a toxicity level that we were ignorant of before. The toxins we have emitted have caused people to stumble, tarnished our Lord's reputation, and made many of our relationships hazardous environments. This is serious business.

In the next chapter we will take up some case studies to show how the process can work. Each of these examples reflects real pastoral counseling situations and sermon material.[4]

CHAPTER 9

Sinful Anger

Our culture has turned anger on its head. We live in an angry society, and someone told us somewhere along the line, "Hey, it's better to let that stuff out than keep it bottled up and then lose it at a fast-food joint or at the Department of Motor Vehicles." There is something in the air that soothes us into thinking that being angry is okay. I mean, who can help getting mad when there is so much to get mad about? The daytime talk-show guru says, "The problem isn't that we get mad; we can't help that. What matters is that we don't hurt anybody." The real issue, when it comes to anger, is not what the afternoon talk-show doctor says, but what the Bible says. With biblical lenses, we need to see anger as it is.

Understanding Anger

Anger is an emotion. It is an internal feeling that manifests itself in a variety of ways. It tells us much about ourselves if we listen. Keep in mind that our emotions not only express our values and evaluations but also influence motives and conduct. So anger is something we *feel* and *do*. Robert Jones is helpful when he says, "Anger is complex. It comprises the whole person and encompasses our whole package of beliefs, feelings, actions and desires."[1]

However, anger is not always sinful. Our capacity to feel anger is actually a part of the image of God in us. God is holy and perfect and yet he can be angry (as we saw in chapter 1). The Lord Jesus was angry on occasion (e.g., Mark 3:5). God is slow to anger and is compassionate (Ps. 103:8). His anger lasts for a moment (Ps. 30:5). He restrains his anger (Ps. 78:38). And yet his anger is a regular theme in Scripture, and sometimes it is described in fierce terms

(Ps. 78:65–66). The conclusion is that not all anger is sinful anger. That is why the apostle commands us, "Be angry and do not sin; do not let the sun go down on your anger" (Eph. 4:26). As a result of the fall, however, it may be safe to say that much if not most of our anger is sinful; thus Paul's caveat, ". . . and do not sin."

Lou Priolo, in his very helpful book *The Heart of Anger*, has a diagram entitled, "Is your anger righteous anger?"[2] He explains that righteous anger occurs when God does not get what he wants. Righteous anger is motivated by a sincere love for God. Righteous anger is aroused when God's will is violated. It is my conviction that this righteous anger is what frequently motivated the writers of the imprecatory psalms as they prayed curses on God's enemies.

Priolo also explains that sinful anger happens when I do not get what I want. It is motivated by a love of some idolatrous desire. It happens when my will is violated, which provokes my anger when *I* am the lord of my life. In the overall balance of our lives, we may have to plead "no contest" when it comes to the kind of anger we experience most. Alec Motyer is probably right on target when he says, "Most of us would have to confess that holy anger belongs to a state of sanctification to which we have not attained."[3]

Inside of Me, Not Outside of Me

Sinful anger is an internal problem, not a circumstantial and external one. Right here is where many of us sinners go wrong. We want to attribute our anger to something outside of ourselves: traffic, a difficult coworker, an uncooperative spouse, a self-willed child, a misbehaving puppy, or a rebellious lawn mower that will not start. But anger is an internal problem; it comes from our own hearts. The Lord Jesus cut it straight when he said, "From within, out of the heart of man, come evil thoughts, sexual immorality, theft, murder, adultery, coveting, wickedness, deceit, sensuality, envy, slander, pride, foolishness. All these evil things come from within, and they defile a person" (Mark 7:21–23).

External circumstances may give occasion for anger to surface, but what comes boiling over the top comes from inside of us, not outside of us. Paul Tripp drives this one home:

> When angry, most people explain their anger by blaming something or someone else outside themselves. . . . James [4:1-10] says we will never understand our anger that way. Instead, he counsels us to do the exact opposite—to look within. This is a fundamental biblical principle. The only way to understand your anger is to examine your own heart.[4]

Try this one in the pastor's study with a married couple who are at each other's throats. It is not a safe truth at times. "Mr. Jawbone, I understand that nobody pushes your buttons like Mrs. Jawbone. But even when she is doing her level-headed best to carefully calculate what buttons should be pushed with the precise pounds per square inch, when you blow up, use profanity, and throw things, your anger comes from your own black heart. She has her sin, but make no mistake about it—the anger is all yours."

The Heating Element of Wrong Thinking

Sinful anger begins with wrong thought processes, i.e., our values and evaluations. The wrong thinking then affects the emotions. Sometimes it may be a Crock-Pot effect, a steady, slow, simmering heat. Sometimes it may be more immediate, more explosive like a violent chemical reaction. But there are certain assumptions, thought patterns, and mental attitudes that undergird our anger— the heating element, if you will. What's cooking on the inside will come out.

An example would be anger that emerges from sinful pride. Proverbs 13:10 says, "By insolence comes nothing but strife, but with those who take advice is wisdom." The New International Version puts it this way: "Pride only breeds quarrels." Pride is a mental attitude based on faulty assumptions about ourselves. The pride that breeds anger usually takes the mask of frustration. The angry person demands that he get his way and expects that others should acquiesce at all times, and when that does not happen he may say, "I am just frustrated! Why can't he . . . Why can't she . . ."

as volcanic ash spews all over the room. The proud man is usually the person who, while demanding forgiveness and forbearance from others, can't spare a gram for anyone else, and in the process angrily condemns those who don't meet his standards or fail to forgive him in a nanosecond.

Anger can also come from *believing* we deserve something or have certain rights. When our just deserts are withheld, postponed, or neglected, or when our rights are violated or denied, we get angry. That is the point of James 4:1–2: "What causes quarrels and what causes fights among you? Is it not this, that your passions are at war within you? You desire and do not have, so you murder. You covet and cannot obtain, so you fight and quarrel. You do not have, because you do not ask." James starts this powerhouse section with a great question: "Why are you fighting? What is the cause?" The answer is devastating: we want and we don't get, so we go on the warpath. We want our own way. We want what we want. We deceive ourselves into thinking we deserve what we want. We have rights to what we want. This is self-deception working its depraved magic. When we don't get what we want (our desires), we get angry (quarrels, fights, murder). Paul Tripp strips it down for us: "Desire lies at the base of every angry feeling, word and action."[5]

What Is Inside Will Come Out

Anger comes out one way or another. As a powerful emotion, it erupts into something we do. The two most common reactions to anger are blowing up or clamming up. Whether it is Cain killing Abel in anger and jealous rage (Gen. 4:4–8) or Ahab pouting like a child over not being able to acquire Naboth's vineyard (1 Kings 21), sinful anger comes out. Whether the manifestation is clamming up, blowing up, withdrawing, or striking out verbally or physically, sinful anger is an ugly, toxic, defiling emotion that leaves destruction in its wake—bad memories, broken relationships, and ruined lives. The irony is that the angry person often justifies the anger.

A husband told me with confidence, "Pastor, I can only get through to her when I am yelling and using profanity."

"Oh, really? And when she finally listens, you are able to do things God's way?" "Exactly!" was his immediate, triumphant reply.

"So you think that your use of anger is justified because it accomplishes God's purpose."

Another triumphant "I told you so," then, "Yes, that's what I am saying."

I said, "I think God's opinion is different from yours. 'For the anger of man does not achieve the righteousness of God'" (James 1:20, NASB).

We are very quick to justify our anger because we think it produces results. This is unbiblical thinking that will prevent us from ever putting sinful anger to death. As long as we think about it unbiblically and justify it wickedly, it will control us, and we will never kill it.

We must see anger as a villain. We must see it is something inside of us, not outside of us. We must see that it usually starts with our pride or sinful values. We must understand that no matter what evidence we see of anger's effectiveness, it is a lie. We must have our eyes and hearts opened to comprehend and feel the sinfulness of sinful anger in all of its biblical ugliness. We need to see it for the terrorist it really is and despise it as God really does. It is this truth alignment that will give us the starting point to put this toxic emotion to death.

A Biblical Sketch of Anger

Anger motivated the first murder in the Bible, an act of fratricide (Gen. 4:3–8). The proverbs repeatedly indict anger as folly (Prov. 14:17, 29; 29:11). Folly is not just some minor character flaw or defect; it is at heart anti-God, self-centered rebellion. The proverbs present sinfully angry people as troublemakers (Prov. 15:18; 29:22), hopeless cases (Prov. 19:19), and dangerously contagious (Prov. 22:24). In the Sermon on the Mount, Jesus teaches us that anger is the very spirit of murder (Matt. 5:21–22). The deeds of flesh, that motley harvest of unregenerate fruit, has its fair share of sins related to anger:

Now the works of the flesh are evident: sexual immorality, impurity, sensuality, idolatry, sorcery, enmity, strife, jealousy, fits of anger, rivalries, dissensions, divisions, envy, drunkenness, orgies, and things like these. I warn you, as I warned you before, that those who do such things will not inherit the kingdom of God. (Gal. 5:19–21)

The apostle Paul warns us that sinful anger can become a base of operations for the Devil in our lives. "Be angry and do not sin; do not let the sun go down on your anger, and give no opportunity to the devil" (Eph. 4:26–27). The "opportunity" is literally a place, that is, a place to stand. Experience exegetes the meaning of this text for us time and time again, especially in marriage and in the church. Robert Jones does not exaggerate when he says, "Unresolved anger and unreconciled relationships further Satan's agenda of shredding the church's unity."[6]

Gaining a biblical perspective on sinful anger should compel us to think biblically about it. The biblical perspective is the infallible instrument panel by which we fly. There are times when it feels good to blow off steam and vent. There are times when we wrongly think our anger is justified or that it achieves a good purpose. All of these unbiblical feelings and thoughts must be brought under the authority of the Word and confessed as sin.

Furthermore, we must confess and repent of our deeds and expressions of anger. We cannot conceal them. This will often require a family meeting, a phone call, or a letter, repenting and asking for forgiveness from those whom we have hurt. Be specific, not general. For husbands and dads this is especially difficult. But it is necessary. Bonhoeffer warns, "It is perilous for the Christian to lie down to sleep with an unreconciled heart."[7]

We must be determined to forsake the anger (Prov. 28:13). We must put it off (Eph. 4:31–32; Col. 3:8–10). In other words, the sinful anger must be something that we want to get rid of like an old, flea-infested, ratty coat. This happens when we begin to think about it the way God thinks about it.

In the place of sinful anger, we need to put on tenderness, compassion, and kindness (Eph. 4:31–32; Col. 3:8–10). This requires some serious work. First, it means we control our thought processes by asking ourselves some tough questions. *How is my pride breeding the anger in my heart? What am I not getting that I am elevating to idol-status and willing to go to war over?* Put these two questions right up front and be courageous enough to ask them. Think through the process. Identify the source. Is it my pride? Is it not getting my way?

This process may require some extra work because, like so many of our sins, sinful anger can become a habitual part of us. In order to get rid of it we may need a more in-depth thought-and-emotions realignment project. Lou Priolo has an anger journal that is very helpful in tracking down wrong thinking that leads to wrong feelings.[8] I would also encourage prayerfully reading, perhaps with an accountability partner, Priolo's book *The Heart of Anger* or Robert Jones's book *Uprooting Anger*. Both are very, very helpful and practical. Commit to memory some texts that are poignantly relevant to your own situation. Pray through them every day as a discipline and be quick to call them to mind when needed.

Once we begin to have a biblical perspective and think properly about sinful anger, we are in a much better place to start exercising self-control. God told Cain he needed to master the anger that was welling up inside (Gen. 4:7). Proverbs exhorts us to put away our anger: "Whoever is slow to anger is better than the mighty, and he who rules his spirit than he who takes a city" (Prov. 16:32). "A man without self-control is like a city broken into and left without walls" (Prov. 25:28). James tells that we are to be slow to anger (James 1:19). Paul tells us to put off anger and put on compassion and kindness (Eph. 4:31–32).

Sinful anger is *our* problem. But God has not left us to be controlled by emotions and outbursts; rather, he has equipped us to handle both feeling and action. Through thinking biblically and absorbing what God says and then prayerfully depending on his grace and Holy Spirit, we can mortify the emotions and exhibitions of sinful anger.

CHAPTER 10

Unforgiveness and Bitterness

Some people will object to classifying unforgiveness as an emotion because forgiveness, they say, is not a feeling but an act. Here is my defense for including it in this section. Emotions are more than feelings; they are the expressions of our values and evaluations that affect motives and conduct. Although I certainly agree that forgiveness is an act, it is also never *just* an act. There is an emotional element to forgiveness, which, hopefully, I will demonstrate. The flipside is that emotional barriers often prevent us from forgiving others. The stink crop of unforgiveness is bitterness, which is an emotion as well. Therefore, in our pursuit to sanctify the emotions we need to deal with unforgiveness and bitterness.

I have often told my fellow pastors that if I preached on forgiveness fifty out of fifty-two weeks in a year, I would hold almost every ear in the auditorium. I am usually corrected by my fellow pastors and told that I could preach it all fifty-two weeks in a year and still hold everyone's ear. The subject hits home and it hits hard! Forgiveness is tough. Anyone who has not wrestled with forgiveness is not conscious. Real injuries, real injustices, real hurts and pain, real sins, and real wrongs happen, and they happen all the time. Forgiveness is an ever-present issue as long as we live with people. The failure to deal with forgiveness produces bitterness, which is a spiritually environmental hazard to everyone around. Hebrews 12:15 warns us of the wreckage: "See to it that no one fails to obtain the grace of God; that no 'root of bitterness' springs up and causes trouble, and by it many become defiled."

Nancy Leigh DeMoss relays the corrosive bitterness that comes from unforgiveness. She quotes from a letter written by a man whose father left him when he was two-years-old. The last few lines tell the story: "The hatred I carried for my daddy wrecked my first marriage, and is threatening my second. I am a shell of a person; I do not have any close relationships."[1] The power of unforgiveness is destructive.

Honest self-evaluation is the place we need to start if we are to put a death grip on the ungodly emotions related to unforgiveness and bitterness (Rom. 12:3). The risk of self-deception is high (Jer. 17:9). We all want to think of ourselves as forgiving people. But let's ask the hard question: *Is there any bitterness in my life toward another person?* If there is, bitterness is the fruit, and unforgiveness is the root.

The Bible says a whole lot about forgiveness, and most of it makes us squirm. Spiritual squirminess usually causes us to be pretty poor theologians, and it makes us exegetical contortionists. But if we let the Bible be a hammer when it's supposed to be a hammer and a healing balm when it's supposed to be a healing balm, then our hearts will be broken and healed according to divine wisdom rather than our own sense of emotional convenience.

Biblical Thinking through a Powerful Parable

The pattern for mortifying ungodly emotions starts with biblical thinking. We need to get our heads straight on the issue, and there is no better place to start than with our Lord's parable in Matthew 18:21–35. It is a great place to start because we connect with Peter's question about forgiveness, and then Jesus tells us a story that is designed to inform and move us into right thinking, right feeling, and right actions.

"Peter came up and said to him, 'Lord, how often will my brother sin against me, and I forgive him? As many as seven times?'" (Matt. 18:21). This question comes in the context of community relationships and sins within the church (vv. 15–20). It is a natural question, and Peter is wondering, "What's the limit, Lord? I mean there *must* be a limit." The rabbinic view held that one might forgive three times, but come the fourth time there is no forgiveness. Peter, feeling large-hearted and generous, suggests seven times. Jesus, never one for quick and easy answers, replies with a bombshell and nukes Peter's perceived large-heartedness, saying. "I do not say to you seven times, but seventy times seven" (Matt. 18:22).

This answer is not a math problem. "Okay, that equals 490 times!" Kistemaker underscores the significance: "Completeness times completeness and completeness."[2] Jesus is telling Peter and us that the way of discipleship is the way of forgiveness. Forgiveness marks those who follow Jesus.

Jesus then tells a parable about the seriousness of forgiveness. The parable unfolds in three acts, showing that all of God's true people have been forgiven for far more than they will ever forgive. Therefore, forgiveness from the heart is the true indication that they have received God's forgiveness and cherish it.

The First Act of Jesus' Parable (Matt. 18:23–27)

"Therefore the kingdom of heaven may be compared to a king who wished to settle accounts with his servants. When he began to settle, one was brought to him who owed him ten thousand talents. And since he could not pay, his master ordered him to be sold, with his wife and children and all that he had, and payment to be made. So the servant fell on his knees, imploring him, 'Have patience with me, and I will pay you everything.' And out of pity for him, the master of that servant released him and forgave him the debt."

A day of reckoning had come when the books were opened and accounts were settled. The slaves who were to appear before the master were, perhaps, those who had leased property to farm. Now their April-fifteenth appointment with the tax man had arrived. One particular slave had to be brought before the master; his debt was 10,000 talents. A conservative estimate by today's economic standards would be in the neighborhood of a billion dollars. The amount, of course, is outside the bounds of reality, but that is the point. What the slave owed was an incalculable amount. The amount is so astronomical in the financial realm that it is unbelievable. But in the realm of God and sin, it is an accurate reflection of the magnitude of our sin against God. The point is the man has no possible way to pay it back.

According to the custom of the day, the master sells the servant, the servant's wife and children, and all the servant's assets. The primary point here is that the man had no way to cover his liabilities. As Morris puts it, "The sale was a gesture, not a settlement. . . . His being sold is no more than punishment."[3] There is no chance of being free. Everything is lost. The scene puts a knot in the pit of our stomach if we read with a little imagination. In an act of absolute desperation the servant does the only thing he can. He falls down on the ground, jettisons any appeal to justice, asks for patience, and then promises the impossible. The master is moved with compassion by the scene and acts graciously.

The analogy in the parable is obvious. The master's compassion reflects God's character. The master does more than the man asks and shows unbelievable magnanimity and abounding mercy. He cancels the debt in its entirety. Again, in the realm of finances, it is an unbelievable turn of events. But in the realm of sin and grace it is an apt portrayal of the greatness of grace.

The Second Act of Jesus' Parable (Matt. 18:28–31)

"But when that same servant went out, he found one of his fellow servants who owed him a hundred denarii, and seizing him, he began to choke him, saying, 'Pay what you owe.' So his fellow servant fell down and pleaded with him, 'Have patience with me, and I will pay you.' He refused and went and put him in prison until he should pay the debt. When his fellow servants saw what had taken place, they were greatly distressed, and they went and reported to their master all that had taken place."

The scene is designed to grip and amaze us. As this servant leaves his master's presence, he should have been so overwhelmed with the profound reality of mercy as to be shouting praises to the master with tears of joy. Instead, he looks for another servant, an equal, a peer, who owed him some money. The amount was 100 denarii, which, although not a small sum, was a pittance compared to what he had owed and had been forgiven. Upon seeing his debtor, he violently grabbed him, threatened his life, and threw him into prison, enforcing the same penalty from which he had just been released. The words that the servant's peer uses are almost identical to the words he himself had just used, which moved the master to pity and forgiveness. But his fellow servant's plea for mercy leaves him unmoved.

The scene is disturbing. The servant sends his peer to the torturers without one shred of mercy. The one who had received mercy now acts with strict justice, revealing a small heart and no understanding of what had been done for him. The fellow servants who see it are deeply disturbed by the event and react by reporting it to the master.

Our Lord, just like Nathan the prophet before King David, is setting up his audience. As we read the words of the parable we shake our heads in disgust and unbelief. "What a fool! How could somebody be so blind, so cruel? Can't he do the math?"

The Third Act of Jesus' Parable (Matt. 18:32–35)

"Then his master summoned him and said to him, 'You wicked servant! I forgave you all that debt because you pleaded with me. And should not you have had mercy on your fellow servant, as I had mercy on you?' And in anger his master delivered him to the jailers, until he should pay all his debt. So also my heavenly Father will do to every one of you, if you do not forgive your brother from your heart."

This is high drama. The lord calls him in, calls him on the carpet, and calls him evil. "You *evil* slave!" Don't miss the significance of this adjective in connection to what he says next. "I forgave you all that debt because you pleaded with me. And should not you have had mercy on your fellow servant, *as* I had mercy on you?" What the master had done to the servant should have been so valued by the servant that he in turn acted in a way that showed he valued mercy. The heart of the parable is we are to act towards others as God has acted towards us.

The scene is not over. The master in the parable experiences righteous wrath. What moved him to wrath? The servant spurned the master's mercy by demanding justice from another. Mercy spurned produced holy, white-hot wrath. The master turns over the servant to the torturers until everything is paid. Since the man had no way to repay, this was a life sentence. The language implies eternal punishment. By demanding justice, the servant cuts himself off from mercy.

That is a chilling parable. But Jesus is not quite done. After the sobering end of the parable, Jesus gives his listeners, including us, the prophetic, "thou art the man" application: "Likewise, my heavenly Father will do to you if you do not forgive your brother from the heart."

Forgive from the Heart

There are two things we must not do with this parable. First, we must not minimize this text and explain it away because we believe in eternal security. Second, we must not miss the emotional element of forgiveness, which our Lord specifically calls attention to when he says, "Forgive your brother from the heart," that is, with all sincerity, all that we are. This passage holds out the wonderful offer of forgiveness to sinners of all shapes and sizes. As Fanny Crosby said:

> The vilest offender, who truly believes,
> That moment from Jesus forgiveness receives!

Nevertheless, the passage also emphasizes a serious threat. God's boundless grace to forgive sin is offered, and his awful wrath against all who would spurn that grace through unforgiveness is threatened. Jesus unambiguously teaches the awful fate of being an unforgiving person. Jesus taught us in what we call the "Lord's Prayer" to pray, "Forgive us our debts, as we also have forgiven our debtors" (Matt. 6:12). He then immediately warns, "For if you forgive others their trespasses, your heavenly Father will also forgive you, but if you do not forgive others their trespasses, neither will your Father forgive your trespasses" (Matt. 6:14–15). D. A. Carson states, "Jesus sees no incongruity in the actions of a heavenly Father who forgives so freely and punishes so ruthlessly, and neither should we."[4] In order for us to think biblically about forgiveness, we must truly believe the threats against unforgiveness.

Why Is Forgiveness So Hard?

Why is it so hard to forgive from the heart? Why is the emotional element so difficult to master? We read the parable, we see the importance of forgiveness, and yet there is often a struggle to forgive others.

If a person is unforgiving, it may be they have never truly embraced the forgiveness of God for their sins, just like the servant. Craig Blomberg writes, "Only those who appropriate God's forgiveness by a life of forgiving others show that they have genuinely accepted his pardon."[5] And Don Carson says, "Those who are forgiven must forgive, lest they show themselves incapable of receiving forgiveness."[6] To that we can add the words of Donald Hagner, who writes, "Disciples are the forgiven who forgive."[7] If people *cannot* forgive, it may be they have never experienced the saving mercy of God in Jesus Christ and the forgiveness of sins.

But we really aren't talking about people who *won't* forgive and *can't* forgive. We are talking about people who struggle emotionally to forgive. Here is one reason for the struggle: the pain, the wounds, the hurt can be so great that there is an emotional barrier, so just when we think we have forgiven an offender, a flood of emotions overwhelms us and we struggle afresh.

There are other reasons. Sometimes we may erroneously think our case is special. What the other person did to us is uniquely bad. For others, frankly, unforgiveness is easier than forgiveness. We grow comfortable with unforgiveness; it becomes a dark companion that justifies our meanness and salves our conscience. We might also be afraid that if we forgive, the injury done to us will be forgotten or minimized. Less nobly, we may not forgive because we want to maintain an advantage over another person, having something to hang over his or her head.

Of all the reasons it is hard to forgive, I believe there is one among God's people that is most predominant. The pain caused from the sin against us can be so great that there is an emotional blockade. Just the thought of the sin brings an avalanche of hurt. Perhaps we have mouthed the words, "I forgive you." But just when we think we have forgiven, a flood of emotions overwhelms us, causing us to doubt the truthfulness of our own words. The wounds seem fresh, the pain is piercing, and the feelings of anger, bitterness, and even revenge come in on us like a blitzkrieg.[8]

Thinking Biblically about Forgiveness and Cutting the Root of Bitterness

Whenever I have counseled or preached on forgiveness, I always cover what forgiveness is not. Too many of God's people struggle with guilt, believing they haven't forgiven somebody, when in reality they are not thinking about biblical forgiveness at all. The following list is adapted from a sermon by John Piper, who borrowed it from the Puritan Thomas Watson.[9]

• Forgiveness does not mean that we treat evil deeds as if they were good. True biblical forgiveness requires that sin be called sin and nothing else.

• Forgiveness is not pretending that what happened to me was somehow not really bad.

• Forgiveness does not mean there cannot be righteous anger at the wrong done and pain caused by the sins of others. There should be righteous anger, without sin (Eph. 4:26).

• Forgiveness does not mean there are not painful consequences for those sins. David is the prime example. God forgave David. David's sin was wiped away. But the consequences remained. If a person sins against us in a way that requires the involvement of law enforcement and the courts, forgiveness does not mean erasing the legal consequences.

• Forgiveness does not look the same when the offender has not repented (Luke 17:3–4). We always have the obligation to release all offenders of their debts *before God* (Luke 23:34). This means we do not hang on to offenses; we do not harbor ill feelings, anger, or bitterness. If the offender does not repent, then forgiveness is not explicitly expressed and reconciliation does not occur (Rom. 12:19).[10]

Forgiveness is freely letting go of the offense, not expecting penance or payment or getting even. This should be clear from the parable. Forgiveness is not counting the sin against the offender anymore (Ps. 130:4; Mic. 7:19). Forgiveness is not bringing up the offense as a point of contention, controversy, or anger (Jer. 31:34; Ps. 103:12). Any time there is an argument that begins with something that happened in 1984, you know there has not been biblical forgiveness. Forgiveness recognizes that God has forgiven the offender and shown mercy and that Christ has paid the penalty for his sin, *and now we do with that sin what God has already done.* ". . . Forgiving one another, as God in Christ forgave you" (Eph. 4:32).

How to Break the Emotional Barrier

Take the Warnings Seriously

The emotional alignment begins by taking seriously the threats of our loving Lord against an unforgiving heart (Matt. 6:12, 14–15; 18:35). The greatest risk of an unforgiving spirit is the loss of heaven. The threats are made to grip the emotions; there is something at stake here we cannot ignore because we think it sounds too much like works or not enough like Jesus. People who will not forgive will not be forgiven. Forgiveness is the lifestyle for the followers of Jesus. As DeMoss reminds us, "Forgiveness is not a method to be learned as much as a truth to be lived."[11]

Keep the Scales of Sin in Perspective

The next aspect of aligning our emotions with biblical truth is the profound realization that comes straight from the parable. All of God's people have been forgiven of far more than we will ever forgive. Therefore, forgiveness from the heart is the true indication that we have received God's forgiveness and cherish it. When we see the majesty and holiness of God, then we see our sins for what they are—unpayable debts against divine holiness. Cherishing God's forgiveness of our billion-dollar debt will compel us to relieve the hundred-dollar debts against us. When we breathe in the air of the cross and the Father's love in wiping away our sins, the last thing in the world we will do is look for the person who owes us a hundred bucks!

Trust in Divine Sovereignty and Justice

Earlier we talked about the oxygen truth of God's character. Here is where we must breathe in deeply the sovereignty of God. Embracing God's sovereignty over our lives and even the pain caused by others can liberate us from bitterness and vengefulness. Joseph modeled this for us in Genesis 50:20: "As for you, you meant evil against me, but God meant it for good, to bring it about that many people should be kept alive, as they are today." This does not relieve people of their moral responsibility, but it frees us to forgive and do them good (see Rom. 12:17–21).

Grab hold of God's sovereignty with one hand and the cross with the other. The sovereignty of God gives teeth to Romans 8:28, "We know that for those who love God all things work together for good, for those who are called according to his purpose." It is the cross that reminds us of our forgiveness (Col. 2:13–14) and then empowers us to forgive others.

Consider the fact that God judged our sins on the cross, and we bear them no more. Justice was satisfied. If those who have sinned against us are in Christ, then their sins, too, have been dealt with at the cross. If they are not in Christ, God will still deal in justice through their eternal punishment. So either on the cross or in hell, all sin will be dealt with by God, and we can leave the ones who have hurt us with him. Romans 12:19 brings it into focus: "Beloved, never avenge yourselves, but leave it to the wrath of God, for it is written, 'Vengeance is mine, I will repay, says the Lord.'"

The power of the cross, the power of grace, the power of the Spirit, and the truth of the Word all work to give us what we need to forgive from the heart. Ultimately, unforgiveness is a matter of unbelief, and forgiveness is a matter of faith. Unforgiveness is unbelief in the gracious forgiveness of God toward us in Christ. Unforgiveness is unbelief in the threats of the Lord Jesus. Unforgiveness is unbelief in his power to provide us with the necessary grace to forgive. Forgiveness flows to others because we cherish by faith what God has done for us; it is supported by faith in the sovereignty of God and is secured by faith in the justice of God.

These truths empower us to forgive from the heart, overcoming the emotional barriers and shriveling the roots of bitterness. John Piper's words are powerful and poignant:

> Saving faith is not merely believing that you are forgiven. Saving faith means believing that God's forgiveness is an awesome thing! Saving faith looks at the horror of sin and then looks at the holiness of God and believes that God's forgiveness is a staggering beauty and unspeakably glorious. Faith in God's forgiveness does not merely mean confidence that I am off the hook. It means confidence that this is the most precious thing in the world. That's why I use the word "cherish." Saving faith cherishes being forgiven by God. And there's the link with the battle against bitterness. You can go on holding a grudge if your faith simply means you are off the hook. But if faith means standing in awe of being forgiven by God, then you can't go on holding a grudge. You have fallen in love with mercy. It's your life. So you battle bitterness by fighting for the faith that stands in awe of God's forgiveness of your sins.[12]

Here is how it works in the life of one man:

> I remember the night. It was the worst of my life. I finally figured it out. She had been unfaithful; she had been lying and it all came out. She had been with another man. I wanted to die. I wanted her to die. I wanted to throw up. She was crying, she was afraid, she was sorry. It was all too much. Her words were frantic. "I am so sorry, please forgive me; please forgive. I understand if you hate me; I don't blame you, but please, please forgive me."
>
> And then it came to me; a revelation of truth gripped my heart. Trembling I said, "I have sinned more against God in one day than you have sinned against me. I forgive you as God in Christ has forgiven me. How could I do otherwise?" It has not been easy. I have struggled a lot with the whole thing. Sometimes it is more difficult than other times. But when my heart grows angry or I hurt all over again, I preach Ephesians 4:32 to myself. I remind myself that God has a purpose in this. Romans 8:28 is true.

She bears her sin no more because Jesus died for it and has washed it away with his precious blood. He has done the same thing with my sin. We have learned to love each other as sinners. We have learned much about grace. It was the truth of God's sovereignty and the power of the cross and the truth of Ephesians 4:32 that saved me from emotional disaster and our marriage from shipwreck.

CHAPTER 11

Fear, Anxiety, and Worry

During seminary days, my wife and I were barely able to make ends meet. We had moved to Portland, Oregon, with some faith but not much money. Jobs were hard to come by, but I was able to get a few janitorial subcontracting accounts, one of which was my "meat and potatoes." It was an eight-hundred-dollar-a-month account at a private school; it might as well have been a million dollars in those days. We paid our rent and utilities and bought our groceries with the income from that account. It was a big account.

One Monday I received a call from the man in charge of this private school. He wanted to talk to my boss and me, and a meeting was set for Thursday of that week. The school had just hired a new principal, and I assumed the meeting was called so we could meet her and discuss some additional cleaning tasks.

Wednesday afternoon I was cleaning the school's library and went to clean the glass on the Xerox machine. As I lifted the lid on the machine, there it was—a contract with another janitorial service, which was owned by the new principal's brother. My anxiety about Thursday's meeting went straight to fear. I looked at the contract and noticed that it underbid our account by almost two hundred dollars a month. My heart sank as I wondered how I was supposed to provide for my wife and two-year-old daughter. Fear gripped me as I faced the certainty of losing the account and the uncertainty of how I could pay rent, let alone buy groceries. Anxiety. Worry. Fear. Real words to depict very real emotions.

Some people have very strong tendencies towards anxiety, worry, and fear. As we come to this section, once again I pluck the same old string on the guitar of mortification: honestly evaluate any sinful emotions, patterns, or tendencies (Rom. 12:3). Be quick to confess and seek to forsake these patterns (Prov. 28:13). There is a subtle danger, however, when it comes to fear, anxiety, and worry. These are not blatantly ugly sins like anger. We can mask these sins under the guise of concern. Let's strip away the fig leaves and own up to anxiety, worry, and fear, whether they characterize our temperaments or we merely succumb to them from time to time.

The Fear of Man and Fear of the Future

"We could list an entire spectrum of feelings under the heading 'fear,' in ascending order or intensity: nervousness . . . worry . . . anxiety . . . terror . . . horror. The difference between them has to do with the intensity of the feeling, not necessarily the seriousness of the problem that evokes the fear. The two do not always match. . . . Worry and fear are first cousins. They vary in intensity but are both forms of the same emotion."[1]

Worry and fear are emotions that overlap. To worry is to feel uneasy or anxious about something. There are troubling thoughts associated with worry. Worry was the emotion I experienced when I received the call Monday to show up for the Thursday appointment. Something important started to slip out of my control.

Anxiety looks like worry amped up a few volts. There is mental and emotional distress. There is an uneasiness of mind caused by uncertainty. I felt this emotion all day Tuesday.

Then there is fear. Fear is the emotion of serious distress, which is aroused by impending danger, evil, or pain, whether real or imagined. Fear makes us feel helpless. Fear hauntingly reminds us we are not in control, and there is nothing we can do about it. Fear is what I felt that Thursday morning. My heart raced. My hands were sweaty. My family's future seemingly rested in someone else's hands, someone who did not care about us one bit.

There is good fear that helps preserve our lives. "I am going too fast. I am too close to the edge. Stop the chain saw; it's making a dangerous sound." There is also the fear of the Lord, which is the heart of godliness (Prov. 1:7; 9:10). But most of the time, the emotions of fear, anxiety, and worry are not legitimate or necessary, but in fact are sinful.

Consider the fear of others, manifested by peer pressure and by being a people pleaser and an approval junkie, controlled by the opinions of others. Fear of others includes an inordinate hunger for attention or relationships, the fear to speak truth, and the fear of rejection. Proverbs 29:25 says, "The fear of man lays a snare, but whoever trusts in the Lord is safe."[2]

There is also fear or anxiety about the future. There is the fear of losing our health, our money, our job, a 401(k), or a relationship. There is also the fear of being hurt, emotionally or physically. There is the fear of getting old, not being able to remember our own name. There is the fear of dying. Our Lord Jesus, in the parable of the sower, said, "As for what was sown among thorns, this is the one who hears the word, but *the cares of the world* and the deceitfulness of riches choke the word, and it proves unfruitful" (Matt. 13:22). He also warned us in Luke 21:34, "But watch yourselves lest your hearts be weighed down with dissipation and drunkenness and *cares of this life*, and that day come upon you suddenly like a trap." David Powlison observes, "If what you *most value* can be taken away or destroyed, then you set yourself up for anxiety."[3]

A Biblical Description of Fear, Worry, and Anxiety

"And which of you by being anxious can add a single hour to his span of life? If then you are not able to do as small a thing as that, why are you anxious about the rest?" (Luke 12:25–26). Among those our Lord addressed were many who subsisted day to day. Jesus spoke to them about the needs of daily life. For such people, you can imagine how easy it would be to worry about the immediate future. Most of us in America cannot relate to that kind of anxiety. Jesus then asked what such anxiety actually accomplishes, and he answers by pointing out that anxiety cannot add a single hour to one's life. In other words, worrying accomplishes absolutely nothing.

This may seem like a no-brainer, but it is an ever-present truth we need to remember. I needed to remember it recently when I received a call with some terrible news on the eve of our all-day elders' and deacons' retreat. One of our church's significant ministries seemed on the brink of collapse because of interpersonal conflict. I heard the words on the phone, "We are done. We can't do this anymore." I hung up and began to worry.

My wife came home from a fundraiser for our Christian school and could tell I was worried. I lay in bed playing all the scenarios through my mind, rehearsing all the words I needed to say. Anxiety filled my heart. Then I thought, "This is accomplishing nothing except robbing me of much-needed rest. It is the Lord's ministry. It is his work." I prayed and went to sleep.

Worry and anxiety not only fail to accomplish anything, they also form a springboard for other problems. Solomon said, "Anxiety in a man's heart weighs him down" (Prov. 12:25). Worry is a crippling emotion that paralyzes us. It bogs us down emotionally, making us virtually useless for anything else. In addition, it leads to other sins. "Fret not yourself; it tends only to evil" (Ps. 37:8b). Isaiah 57:11 catalogues some of those sins for us: "Whom did you dread and fear, so that you lied, and did not remember me, did not lay it to heart? Have I not held my peace, even for a long time, and you do not fear me?" Fear leads to lying, forgetting God, not trusting God, and not fearing God. John Piper expands on the evil associates of anxiety:

> In the decades that have followed I have learned much more about the fight against anxiety. I have learned, for instance, that anxiety is a condition of the heart that gives rise to many other sinful states of mind. Think for a moment how many different sinful actions and attitudes come from anxiety. Anxiety about finances can give rise to coveting and greed and hoarding and stealing. Anxiety about succeeding at some task can make you irritable and abrupt and surly. Anxiety about relationships can make you withdrawn and indifferent and uncaring about other people. Anxiety about how someone will respond to you can make you cover the truth and lie about things. So if anxiety could be conquered, a mortal blow would be struck to many other sins.[4]

The Bible clearly forbids sinful fear, anxiety, and worry. The commands "do not fear" and "do not be afraid" appear almost one hundred times in the Bible. Some of the passages are not only classic texts on not fearing but also stalwart promises telling us *why* we should not fear. "Fear not, for I am with you; be not dismayed, for I am your God; I will strengthen you, I will help you, I will uphold you with my righteous right hand" (Isa. 41:10). "For I, the LORD your God, hold your right hand; it is I who say to you, 'Fear not, I am the one who helps you.' Fear not, you worm Jacob, you men of Israel! I am the one who helps you, declares the LORD; your Redeemer is the Holy One of Israel" (Isa. 41:13–14). The Lord Jesus in the Sermon on the Mount gives the ultimate word forbidding worry and anxiety:

> Therefore I tell you, do not be anxious about your life, what you will eat or what you will drink, nor about your body, what you will put on. Is not life more than food, and the body more than clothing? Look at the birds of the air: they neither sow nor reap nor gather into barns, and yet your heavenly Father feeds them. Are you not of more value than they? And which of you by being anxious can add a single hour to his span of life? And why are you anxious about clothing? Consider the lilies of the field, how they grow: they neither toil nor spin, yet I tell you, even Solomon in all his glory was not arrayed like one of these. But if God so clothes the grass of the field, which today is alive and tomorrow is thrown into the oven, will he not much more clothe you, O you of little faith? Therefore do not be anxious, saying, 'What shall we eat?' or 'What shall we drink?' or 'What shall we wear?' For the Gentiles seek after all these things, and your heavenly Father knows that you need them all. But seek first the kingdom of God and his righteousness, and all these things will be added to you. Therefore do not be anxious about tomorrow, for tomorrow will be anxious for itself. Sufficient for the day is its own trouble." (Matt. 6:25–34)
>
> "Fear not, little flock, for it is your Father's good pleasure to give you the kingdom." (Luke 12:32)

The apostle Paul is equally clear. "Rejoice in the Lord always; again I will say, Rejoice. Let your reasonableness be known to everyone. The Lord is at hand; do not be anxious about anything, but in everything by prayer and supplication with thanksgiving let your requests be made known to God (Phil. 4:4–6).

We live with the constancy of the unknown. We are all prone to worry and anxiety. We live in a scary world. We are prone to fear. Whether we are the proverbial "worry wart" or wrestle only when the biggies come, we all struggle with fear, anxiety, and worry. These emotions can be stifling, suffocating, and even paralyzing. In order to control them and conquer them, we need to know the source.

The Source of Fear, Anxiety, and Worry

We might be tempted to think the emotions of fear, worry, and anxiety are truly emotions that come from outside of us. After all, we live in a post-9/11 world. We live in a world with a wicked Devil on the prowl (1 Pet. 5:8). We live in a world that is fallen, riddled with sin, sickness, death, and disaster. So if any emotions were to come from outside us, victimizing us, surely it must be the emotions of fear, anxiety, and worry. But before we go there, let's remember our emotions express our values and evaluations. Our emotions tell us what we really, *really* believe. Therefore, not even fear, worry, and anxiety can be attributed to something that happens to us.

The Bible leaves us no room for debate. The source of fear, worry, and anxiety is unbelief. The unbelief is specific, spelled out for us by Isaiah and Jesus. When we fail to believe that God is for us, will take care of us, has our future in his hands, and is with us right now, we cave in to fear, worry, or anxiety.

Listen again to the prophet: "Whom did you dread and fear, so that you lied, and *did not remember me*, did not lay it to heart? Have I not held my peace, even for a long time, and you do not fear me?" Likewise, what is our Lord's diagnosis of the anxiety shown in Matthew 6:25–34? The answer is, "O you of little faith" (6:30). When we are gripped with anxiety and fear, we are making an evaluation. Our souls are speaking, and our innermost being is expressing what we believe and whom we do not believe. How do we handle these emotions that can overwhelm us? We put a stranglehold on them with the vise grips of truth.

Biblical Bullets for Handling Fear, Anxiety, and Worry

The sovereign king of the entire universe is our Father. He has not only created us, but he has also recreated us in Jesus Christ and has provided everything we need. Paul tells the timid Timothy, "For God has not given us a spirit of fear, but of power and of love and of a sound mind" (2 Tim. 1:7, NKJV). Unbelieving, sinful fear is contrary to what God has put in us at conversion (Rom. 8:15). We overcome the grip of fear by knowing what God has done for us and in us through his Son. We break fear's grip by realizing God did not give this fear to us; rather, he has given us the spirit of power, love, and self-control.

We also squeeze the life out of fear, worry, and anxiety by utilizing truths such as that found in Proverbs 18:10: "The name of the LORD is a strong tower; the righteous man runs into it and is safe." Once again, we return to the oxygen truth of God's character. When the emotional hurricane winds of fear, anxiety, and worry assail us, we run into God and his character, his nature, and his attributes, like someone would run into a strong tower seeking refuge from a storm. Our Father has provided all that he is for our safety. When we are focused on him we are assured that we are safe, and we no longer fear. Safety calms our fears. The psalmist reiterates this for us: "When I am afraid, I put my trust in you" (Ps. 56:3).

Another death knell to fear, worry, and anxiety is the confidence that God is working out the details of our lives, which may be scary right now, for our good and ultimate conformity to the image of his Son (Rom. 8:28–29). We fight fear, worry, and anxiety with faith in God's promises and with confidence in his truth. As our minds are renewed with the promises of his Word, we find an emotional security. "In God I trust; I shall not be afraid. What can man do to me?" (Ps. 56:11).

This is the connection that David makes: "The LORD is my light and my salvation; whom shall I fear? The LORD is the stronghold of my life; of whom shall I be afraid? When evildoers assail me to eat up my flesh, my adversaries and foes, it is they who stumble and fall. Though an army encamp against me, my heart shall not fear; though war arise against me, yet I will be confident" (Ps. 27:1–3).

Were there external threats? Was there impending danger? Did the circumstances shout, "You are helpless"? Of course. The list is indisputable: evildoers assailing to eat up his flesh, adversaries, foes, armies encamped around him for his destruction. All the circumstances said, "You are not in control."

What does David do? He focuses on the character of God. He says, in essence, "Yahweh [God's covenant name reflecting covenant faithfulness] is my light and salvation.[5] He is the stronghold of my life, that is, my strength and my protection from danger. The conclusion is I will not fear anyone, I will not fear, period. I will be confident in him."

The psalmist again says, "When the cares of the heart are many, your consolations delight my soul" (Ps. 94:19). In other words, he is saying, "I overcome anxiety by focusing on the consolations, the promises, you have given me in your Word." The psalmist again calls to the saints, "Rest in the Lord and wait patiently for Him; Do not fret because of him who prospers in his way, Because of the man who carries out wicked schemes" (Ps. 37:7, nasb). Rest equals trusting in who God is and what he has promised to be for us. Resting gives power to stop fretting. Trusting provides the platform of emotional stability and strength. "Cast your burden on the Lord, and he will sustain you; he will never permit the righteous to be moved" (Ps. 55:22; cf. 1 Pet. 5:7).

Promise after promise is designed to kill fear and neutralize anxiety and worry. God's promises kill fear because they remind us who God is and what he is like, that he is near us, and that we find our security and peace in him. "I sought the Lord, and he answered me and delivered me from all my fears" (Ps. 34:4). We obey the commands by faith and own the promises through prayer, and we experience his peace. "Do not be anxious about anything, but in everything by prayer and supplication with thanksgiving let your requests be made known to God. And the peace of God, which surpasses all understanding, will guard your hearts and your minds in Christ Jesus" (Phil. 4:6–7).

On that overcast Thursday morning, I sat on the steps outside the office waiting for the appointment. My fear was dissipating as

I recited to myself and prayed through Isaiah 41:10: "Fear not, for I am with you; be not dismayed, for I am your God; I will strengthen you, I will help you, I will uphold you with my righteous right hand." I preached to myself and prayed, "God is with me; I do not need to fear. God is my God; I do not need to be anxious. God promises to strengthen me; I will get through this. God promises to help me and uphold me. We will not starve or be left destitute."

The meeting happened. I lost the account. I was blamed for "not doing a good enough job," although I knew the real reason we lost the contract was that we were underbid. But that was okay. I was able to share Isaiah 41:10 with Ariel. I told her how God had helped me and delivered me from my fear. We gave thanks together and rejoiced that our God is the God of gods, who loves his children, is present with his children, and protects and provides for his children. What can man do to us? We will not be afraid. By the way, God gave me a better job that got us through seminary without having to scratch and scrape to make ends meet.

CHAPTER 12

Depression

As a pastor, I take depression very seriously. We lost a young woman in our congregation to suicide during a prolonged depression. More than once, I have been in the hospital ER due to failed suicide attempts of depressed persons. Only a worthless physician doubts the pain, darkness, helplessness, and hopelessness of those who suffer from depression. It is a dangerous physician who throws a few Bible verses at those who are depressed and tells them just to have more faith.

As I approach this final chapter on mortifying ungodly emotions, I want to deal with depression as sensitively and biblically as I can. Depression is complex. The medical and physiological issues are complex. The emotional and spiritual issues are complex. We will focus on some basics, and hopefully I will provide some biblical principles to deal with some facets of depression.[1]

Depression Described in the Bible

In the book of Deuteronomy God promises a number of covenant curses for covenant unfaithfulness. He tells his people:

> Among these nations you shall find no respite, and there shall be no resting place for the sole of your foot, but the LORD will give you there a trembling heart and failing eyes and a languishing soul. Your life shall hang in doubt before you. Night and day you shall be in dread and have no assurance of your life. In the morning you shall say, "If only it were evening!" and at evening you shall say, "If only it were morning!" because of the dread that your heart shall feel, and the sights that your eyes shall see. (Deut. 28:65–67)

This is not a clinical definition of depression. However, the description in the text describes what we would call depression: no rest, trembling heart, despair of soul, life hanging in doubt, fearing day and night, no assurance, no security, a dread of the morning, hating the thought of facing the day, a dread of night, shrinking from the thought of trying to sleep. The cause of these symptoms is what the heart feels and what the eyes see ahead. Anyone who has felt depression can identify with some if not most of that description.

The Psalms, as we have noted, cover the whole spectrum of human experience. The lament psalms, in particular, deal with what we could legitimately call depression. In Psalms 42 and 43, which were probably originally one psalm, the psalmist uses a mournful refrain, which he repeats three times: "Why are you cast down, O my soul, and why are you in turmoil within me? Hope in God; for I shall again praise him, my salvation" (Pss. 42:5, 11; 43:5). The psalmist asks himself why he is downcast or in despair (a depression-oriented word) and has inner turmoil (another depression-oriented word). The repetition of this refrain is powerful and haunting but also hopeful. For now, notice the words *despair*, *turmoil*, and *downcast*.

Later, the psalmist appears overcome with what Welch calls "a stubborn darkness." We read, "Will the Lord spurn forever, and never again be favorable? Has his steadfast love forever ceased? Are his promises at an end for all time? Has God forgotten to be gracious? Has he in anger shut up his compassion?" (Ps. 77:7–9). If this is not the language of depression, then I don't know what is. The darkness, which has closed in, begins to taunt the depressed soul with horrible thoughts about God. "God is spurning you! He does not care about you. He might love others, but he does not love you. His covenant love for you is done, over with! His promises for you have all run out. God no longer has any compassion for you. He is angry with you."

The proverbs also describe depression. "Hope deferred makes the heart sick" (Prov. 13:12). "A joyful heart is good medicine, but a crushed spirit dries up the bones" (Prov. 17:22). "A man's spirit will endure sickness, but a crushed spirit who can bear?" (Prov.

18:14). Dashed hopes, a sick heart, a crushed spirit, and dried-up bones all relate to the depressed state. The death of hope can sap the very life from us, crushing us. "To live without hope is to live without a future. . . . Those who are depressed try to kill it because it has betrayed them. . . . Without hope, you feel like the walking dead."[2]

Beyond descriptions of depression in the Bible, we also encounter some biblical figures who experienced depression. Consider Job. Read the book through, follow the units of discourse, listen to Job. He is sarcastic; he is full of self-pity. He is at times the walking wounded; at other times he is the walking dead. There is a flame of faith in Job, but for the most part it burns low. Consider Elijah, who went quickly from the spiritual heights of Mount Carmel to the depths under the juniper tree. He was so depressed he wanted to die (1 Kings 19:4).

Jonah was in the same boat (no pun intended). His hopes had been dashed by the repentance of the Ninevites. He really wanted to see them become the cannon fodder of God's judgment for all the horrible things they had done to his people. Instead, God used his preaching to bring about their repentance, and as a result he wanted to die (Jonah 4:3, 8). Even the resilient, indefatigable apostle Paul, as we examined earlier, came to a point in his life where he was over his head emotionally and physically. He despaired of life and saw death as his only prospect (2 Cor. 1:8–10).

The Signs of Depression

When we talk about depression, we are talking about certain feelings. These feelings are not always easy to define, but here is a brief overview.[3] Depression is marked by feelings of despair and hopelessness. There can also be emotional pain, not like a headache or a sprained ankle, but a gnawing pain that is felt virtually everywhere. Emotional numbness may be another symptom. The numbness is a sense of indifference, not caring about anyone or anything. Ironically, the pain and the numbness may coexist. Depression may also leave a person with no energy and no normal desires (such as for sexual intimacy or eating). Depression may cause insomnia, excessive sleep, weight loss, and fatigue.

A paralyzing dread of the future may be another sign of depression, for instance, a fear of the holidays. Depression may cause the sufferer to have a difficult time concentrating or keeping his thoughts in order. Oftentimes depression can bring about restlessness. Thoughts of death are also common. Suicidal thoughts and even planning the deed can occupy the depressed person. There can also be feelings of guilt, anxiety, anger, and fear for no apparent reason.

Depression should not be taken lightly. It is a destroyer. It does not look the same in every person; it is not manifest to the same degree. It is a terrible mistake not to take it seriously. It is also a mistake to believe you know what depressed people mean when they say they are depressed. Those who have never been depressed frequently do not understand the darkness of depression, so they get frustrated with those experiencing it. They wonder why they can't just pull themselves out of it. As one who believes in the sufficiency of God's Word and the power of the Holy Spirit, I also realize that depression is not a matter of "take two verses, pray, and call me in the morning."

The Sources of Depression

The Bible distinguishes between the body and the soul (Matt. 10:28). It also affirms the interpenetration and interdependence between the body and the soul (e.g., Ps. 38:3). It should not surprise us that physical problems can lead to both depression and spiritual problems, and spiritual problems can lead to depression and physical problems. Some physical sources of depression might include prolonged illness, childbirth, surgery, hormonal changes, changes in diet, and fatigue.[4] Many other physical factors may also contribute to depression. The important point to remember as we proceed is that we are body-soul creatures.

There are also spiritual sources of depression. The most common spiritual source is the guilt caused by sin. Psalm 32 weaves together the spiritual, emotional, and physical threads:

For when I kept silent, my bones wasted away
through my groaning all day long.
For day and night your hand was heavy upon me;
my strength was dried up as by the heat of summer.
I acknowledged my sin to you,
and I did not cover my iniquity;
I said, "I will confess my transgressions to the Lord*,"*
and you forgave the iniquity of my sin. (Ps. 32:3–5)

The root cause of the psalmist's depression is unconfessed sin. The results were physical depletion, guilt, and emotional heaviness. Even more graphic is Psalm 38:1–10:

O Lord*, rebuke me not in your anger,*
nor discipline me in your wrath!
For your arrows have sunk into me,
and your hand has come down on me.
There is no soundness in my flesh
because of your indignation;
there is no health in my bones
because of my sin.
For my iniquities have gone over my head;
like a heavy burden, they are too heavy for me.
My wounds stink and fester
because of my foolishness,
I am utterly bowed down and prostrate;
all the day I go about mourning.
For my sides are filled with burning,
and there is no soundness in my flesh.
I am feeble and crushed;
I groan because of the tumult of my heart.
O Lord, all my longing is before you;
my sighing is not hidden from you.
My heart throbs; my strength fails me,
and the light of my eyes—it also has gone from me.

The interpenetration between sin, guilt, depression, and spiritual and physical effects is astonishing. We cannot discount the depressive power of guilt that comes from sin. As a thirteen-year-old boy raised in a Catholic home, I was eaten up with guilt because of my sin. I went to confession and did my penance, but nothing brought relief. I hated the morning because I had to face the day, and I hated the night because it meant being alone with myself, my thoughts, and God. God saved me through faith in Christ and delivered me from my guilt and consequential depression. My pastoral observation is that people who suffer from depression frequently (not always) have sin-related issues that have not been resolved through confession and repentance.

Depression can also occur because of the grief of losing a loved one, losing a job, or some major life change. Stress over children, marriage, and finances can also spin us out of control emotionally, landing us in depression. Behind much of this activity is the enemy of our souls, the Devil. "Satan is attracted to the inward-turning instincts of depression."[5] Satan can use times of depression as an opportunity for an all-out assault on our faith and confidence in God. He can use the "dark nights of the soul" to cast doubt on the goodness and love of God.

Depression has some very serious liabilities. Much of the time when depression hits, depressed people move to self-pity. They can become consumed with their pain and darkness. They can become absorbed with themselves. Another liability is the very real possibility of developing certain depression patterns. The holidays, PMS, and anniversaries of painful events can begin to set us up to expect depression. If we expect it to come, it will come.

Those suffering from depression can also fall prey to a downward spiral of thinking and acting. Depressed people will typically try to respond to the depression in one way or another. For some this means overeating, drug use, alcohol abuse, anger, overwork, or neglecting responsibilities. All such responses speed up the downward spiral because they add to the guilt, deepen the pit, and heighten the sense of hopelessness.

One of the saddest liabilities of depression is that it can become a tortuous companion that begins to shape our identity. The thought of living without the depression can become difficult, even frightening. In the course of pastoral counseling, I have observed those who embrace the dark companionship of depression because they are afraid that if they get over it, they will lose something they have come to value. It can look like this: "If the depression goes away, then maybe the grief will go away. If the grief goes away, maybe I won't love my child or friend or spouse as much as I do now." Or it can look like this: "If the depression goes away, maybe the guilt will go away. If the guilt goes away then I won't be sorry for my abortion, my adultery."

Dealing with Depression

Do Not Forget the Temple

We cannot ignore the connection between the body and the soul. A simple step that might help is to take care of the body God gave us. Exercise, good diet, and sleep are ways we can take care of the temple (1 Cor. 6:19–20). Even Paul told Timothy, "Bodily training [exercise] is of some value" (1 Tim. 4:8). Normally we jump to the "littleness" of the value of exercise in order to discount the need for it. Paul's point is not to dismiss bodily exercise. He did not say it was of no value; it is just small in value compared to godliness.

A change of diet might also prove helpful. Our fast-food culture is turning our bodies into toxic waste dumps, making us unhealthy. A healthy diet and exercise can be means of grace to us physically and emotionally. It bears repeating that we are not disembodied spirits. We are body-soul creatures, and how we treat the body can affect the soul.

There is also no shame in seeing a competent medical doctor about our depression. We need some discernment here, because many in the medical field ask a few questions and then write a prescription for a psychotropic drug. But a sensitive doctor can run a blood panel and other tests, checking for certain physical deficiencies known to cause depression.[6] He may also ask the right physiological questions that might lead to some insight and help.

The *Self-Confrontation Manual* wisely advises, "It is important that a medical diagnosis be made by a primary care physician and medical supervision be maintained with some of these conditions. At the same time, however, you must make biblical changes in your life so that you learn to live biblically in the midst of physical need and medical treatment."[7]

What about antidepressant medications? This is a controversial and complex issue and one that requires great care. Although our society makes many assumptions about depression and medication, there is a tremendous amount of uncertainty and theorizing. One should be fully informed about antidepressants or any other psychiatric drugs.[8] One of the possible dangers of taking such drugs is that a person can become dependent on them. Dependence on the medication can become a substitute for dependence on God. Once we put our hope in a prescription instead of the God who raises the dead, we have become idolaters.[9]

There are no easy, cut-and-dried answers when it comes to medication. This is a sensitive and controversial area. There are physical, emotional, and spiritual dangers to consider. Careful research and thorough consultation with a competent doctor and a biblically oriented pastor is highly recommended.

Deal with the Soul

If we look at depression as an emotional problem that is related only to physical factors, then we are practical atheists. Much depression is spiritually related. Some depression is physically related. Much depression is probably both, and trying to decipher the root cause is like trying to unravel the proverbial Gordian knot. The following biblical principles are critical for all of us, and in many cases may prove to be the ropes of truth that pull us from the pit and the emotional rivets that resecure our moorings.

First, we must deal with any known sin. Psalm 32 makes this a biblical requirement. We need to ask the Lord honestly to search our hearts (Ps. 139:23–24). There may be certain sins we have failed to deal with, and the Lord is simply disciplining us until we come to a place of confession and repentance (Psalms 32; 51; Prov. 28:13;

1 John 1:9). It may be unforgiveness, bitterness, resentment, or secret sins we have not been willing to repent of. There may be idols in our hearts we have not had the courage to identify and smash. There may be right eyes and right hands that need to be plucked out or amputated (Matt. 5:29–30). Ed Welch's insight is crucial.

> Compassion cannot ignore unbelief or sin. Too often, family and friends think the depressed person is very fragile and cannot handle any frank discussion about sin or hard-heartedness. But to ignore these issues when they are obvious in someone's life is to treat that person without love and compassion.... The Bible always portrays our sin problem as being deeper than any pain we experience. To ignore sin, especially when it is obvious, is to offer only a very superficial kind of love and compassion, and to withhold help that is needed at the deepest level.[10]

Take Every Thought Captive with Truth

Depression can be cruel. It is an emotional state that makes us vulnerable to believing lies. We combat lies with truth. We overpower wrong feelings with right thinking. This is not some naïve approach that assumes a verse or two will do the trick. But how can we underestimate the power of the Word? It is the Word that can revive and give hope.

A depressed person does not need to hear about his or her counselor's depression; he needs to hear truth. If there is guilt, he needs to hear cross-centered truth and gospel promises (e.g., Rom. 8:1). If there is a troubled heart, he needs to hear Christ's call to trust him and his Father (John 14:1). If there is chaos and confusion because of various troubles, he needs to hear the peace Jesus promised (John 16:33). There are numerous principles in Scripture that deal with suffering and its purpose (James 1:2–4). There are many psalms that are relevant and powerful and honest. We need to learn that the rock for the depressed is the Word (2 Cor. 10:3–5).

We need to preach the powerful truths of the Word to ourselves.[11] This is what the psalmist does in Psalms 42 and 43. He not only questions himself, but he preaches hope in God to himself. "Hope in God; for I shall again praise him, my salvation and my God (Pss. 42:5–6,

11; 43:5). Welch notes, "Wise counsel tells us that we must talk to depression—fight it—rather than merely listen to it."[12] Martyn Lloyd-Jones's words on preaching to yourself are truly a classic:

> Have you realized that most of your unhappiness in life is due to the fact that you are listening to yourself instead of talking to yourself? . . . You must take yourself in hand, you have to address yourself, you have to preach to yourself, question yourself . . . then you must go on to remind yourself of God, Who God is, and what God is and what God has done and what God has pledged Himself to do.[13]

Change Feelings by Doing the Right Thing

This is not easy, but it is biblical. When Cain's countenance fell with anger and jealousy, God's counsel to him was, "If you do well, will you not be accepted? And if you do not do well, sin is crouching at the door. Its desire is for you, but you must rule over it" (Gen. 4:7). In other words, Cain was to do something; he was to do the right thing. *The power often comes in the doing.* Stop the self-pity and do what you are supposed to do. That might mean clean the kitchen. That might mean doing your devotions even if you don't feel like it.

There is something deeper here that needs exploration. It is not merely a matter of doing; it may be a matter of doing for others. Getting outside of ourselves and serving may break the back of the depressed emotions. This struck me with great force as I taught through Isaiah. Look carefully at these words:

> *If you pour yourself out for the hungry*
> *   and satisfy the desire of the afflicted,*
> *then shall your light rise in the darkness*
> *   and your gloom be as the noonday.*
> *And the LORD will guide you continually*
> *   and satisfy your desire in scorched places*
> *   and make your bones strong;*
> *and you shall be like a watered garden,*
> *   like a spring of water,*
> *   whose waters do not fail.* (Isa. 58:10–11)

Wholehearted service for others in need has some astonishing results: light rises in darkness and gloom gives way to the noonday sun. The scorched, parched, and weakened place of depression is replaced with satisfaction and strength, pictured as a garden that is replenished with unfailing springs of water.

A close friend who can sit with us, pray with us, and remind us of what we need to hear can be a means of grace in the darkness. We need the friend who loves at all times (Prov. 17:17), who can stick closer than a brother (Prov. 18:24) and encourage us to fight the depression which threatens our faith (Heb. 3:12–13). We need one who will speak truth in love (Eph. 4:15). The emotional carnage of depression can be controlled and even mortified with the sword of the Spirit (Eph. 6:17).

Depression can be a life-controlling, destructive emotional state. But the Word of God can be the hammer that shatters the lies of depression. The Word can also be the healing balm that salves depression's destructive emotional wounds.

Real Hope through the Word

Years ago I used to teach theology courses at a local Bible school. After class one evening, a young man approached me and asked for an appointment. He was a tall, good-looking, athletic, academically gifted young man who had grown up in a Christian home. Now engaged to be married, he worked as a CPA and taught high-level tennis lessons, and he had aspirations for ministry. We sat down, and for the next hour I listened to his heart-wrenching story of debilitating depression. Darkness, uncertainty, anger, fear, shame, inner turmoil, and chaos overwhelmed him. He had suffered from this depression for years. He had sought professional help. He was scared. Nothing seemed to help, and he was about to get married. How could he bring a new wife into his murky world of depression? He did not know what to do.

I still remember my own eyes welling up with tears as he communicated an emotional pain that I was personally unfamiliar with. My first reaction was, "I am way out of my depth here. This guy needs more than I can give him." The problem was that he had already been to the professionals. He wanted my help. I asked him some questions about his own conversion and walk with the Lord. There was nothing suspect in his profession of faith. Everything seemed to be in place. I told him quite honestly that all I had to offer him was the Word, prayer, and friendship.

As we came to the end, I said, "You know the book report due next month for class? I want you to read a book that isn't in the syllabus. I want you to read Martyn Lloyd-Jones's *Spiritual Depression*. After you read it, come back to my study and we can talk about it." He thanked me, we prayed, and he left.

After each class he would say, "I am enjoying the book." I would say, "I am praying for you." He finished the book and came back. With tears, he explained point by point how God used the truth in the book to confront wrong thinking, weak theology, and low views of God. He was confident God was doing something.

After the semester, we met again. It was nearly twelve weeks after our first appointment. Again he reiterated the impact the book had on him. It was truth he needed to hear; it was truth he needed to own. In the process, God brought him out of the depression and gave him an emotional stability that lasts to this day, almost eight years later. He is a husband, a father, and a seminary student who is thriving as he walks with God in truth.

Part 4

Cultivating
Godly Emotions

CHAPTER 13

An Introduction to Cultivating Godly Emotions

We live in northwestern Nevada, on the eastern side of the Sierras. Although it is beautiful, it is high desert. There is a rose garden in our front yard, and it takes work. We have to stay on top of the weeds or we are inundated with unwanted, life-sucking, ugly, curse-reminders. We must pull the weeds. But there is more to maintaining a rose garden than just pulling the weeds; there is another process called cultivation. Cultivation demands our drip system work properly to water the rose bushes. Cultivation requires pruning at the right time in the right places. Cultivation also means the use of Ortho RosePride flower and rose fertilizer. It is not enough to kill weeds; we need to cultivate the garden. The Christian life is the same way.

Watering, Pruning, and Fertilizing Required

Scripture compares our lives to a garden (Prov. 24:30–34). In Proverbs a slacker owns the garden. "I went by the field of a slacker and by the vineyard of a man lacking sense" (HCSB). There is no cultivation of the garden, so thorns, thistles, and weeds overrun it. The sluggard's lack of cultivation makes him clueless to the fact that the wall, designed for the protection of the garden, has fallen down. The place is a mess. There is no mortification and no cultivation.

Frequently we think of sanctification only in terms of putting to death our sins (Rom. 8:13). We often think, "If only I could root this sin out of my life, then I would be more holy." Putting sins to death is like pulling weeds. It must be done. We cannot allow the noxious, life-draining weeds to grow or they threaten our life and health. But if we stop with pulling up the weeds of sin, we miss a huge part of the Christian life.

Cultivation is the other part. We need to bring certain graces to life by watering, pruning, and even fertilizing. We are to bear the fruit of the Spirit (Gal. 5:22–23; cf. Ps. 37:3). This is cultivation. We are not only to put off certain sins, but we are to put on Christlike virtues and graces (Eph. 4:22–32; 2 Pet. 1:5–7). We must flee sin, but we must also "pursue righteousness, godliness, faith, love, steadfastness, gentleness" (1 Tim. 6:11). This is cultivation.

Cultivation applies to our emotional life. We must pull up the sinful emotions by the roots. They need to be put off and put to death, which is what we have been focusing on in these last few chapters. But there are also godly emotions that must be brought to life. They need to be fanned into flame, put on, pursued, and cultivated. Sam Williams summarizes the process: "Our emotional states are windows into our souls, revealing the allegiance of our hearts. Let us endeavor to think God's thoughts after Him, conform our actions to His Word, and experience emotions that reflect and honor Him."[1]

An Overview

We cannot forget our foundation. As was emphasized in chapter 2, Jesus Christ is God incarnate, and we look to him as the perfect representation of our heavenly Father (John 14:9; 2 Cor. 4:4; Col. 1:15). The Son of God demonstrates every emotion we should have. Jesus Christ is also perfect humanity. He has no sin, defect, or flaw in his character (Heb. 7:26). We look to our Lord Jesus who perfectly possesses and displays the full spectrum of human emotions, without any darkness. We see in our Father and our Savior the goodness of emotions and the godly pattern of emotions.

We are going to invest some significant space to examining our Lord Jesus as the pattern for our own emotional life.[2] Then we will explore certain spiritual disciplines and their relationship to the development of godly emotions. The hope is that, by God's grace, we can begin to cultivate godly emotions that bring us into greater conformity with our Lord Jesus Christ.

CHAPTER 14

Jesus Our Pattern, Part 1

In evangelical circles we spend a tremendous amount of time studying and defending the deity of Christ. This is right and necessary since there are cults and theological liberals who attempt to deny our Lord's deity. But sometimes in our zeal to emphasize one point of theology, we neglect another, which is why in our efforts to defend Christ's deity we have often overlooked the vital doctrine of his humanity.

The Humanity of Our Lord

In the incarnation, our Lord took to himself a real human body and a real human soul. He became a complete human being. He became flesh (John 1:14). He partook of blood and flesh (Heb. 2:14). Jesus was not a deified human or a humanified god. He is fully God and fully man. His full and undiminished humanity is a nonnegotiable article of classic orthodox Christian theology. We cannot deny the real and full humanity of Jesus and still call ourselves Christians (1 John 4:1–2; 2 John 7).

The one component of our Lord's humanity that separates him from the rest of us is his sinless perfection (Heb. 2:17; 4:15; 7:26-27; 2 Cor. 5:21; 1 Pet. 2:21–22). Our Lord not only lived a life free from sin, he also lived a perfect life which was the beautiful portrayal of all that humanity was called to be. Jesus is man as man ought to be (Heb. 2:5–8).[1] Jesus, as perfect humanity, experienced and displayed the full range of human emotions without any sin. B. B. Warfield wrote in his classic essay, "It belongs to the truth of our Lord's humanity that He was subject to all sinless emotions."[2]

Jesus, Our Example

I get a little nervous when I hear people talking about Jesus as our moral example. When the WWJD craze was going full-throttle a number of years ago, I would remind our congregation that WWJD could be a motto for theological liberals as well. Classic liberalism had turned Jesus into a *mere* moral model. Turning Jesus into a *mere* moral model is a failure to appreciate him as the *ultimate* example for us. Jesus is always more than our moral example, but he is never less.

Trying to follow Jesus as our example without his saving power is not only doomed to failure, but it does not honor our Lord in his chief mission, which was to seek and save the lost (Luke 19:10).

The goal of God's saving activity in Jesus Christ is that God's glory is put on display in our being conformed to the image of his Son. Conformity to the image of Christ is God's goal in our predestination: "For those whom he foreknew he also predestined to be conformed to the image of his Son, in order that he might be the firstborn among many brothers" (Rom. 8:29). Conformity to the image of Christ is the goal of our sanctification: "Put on the new man, who is being renewed in knowledge according to the image of his Creator" (Col. 3:10, HCSB; cf. 2 Cor. 3:18; Gal. 4:19).[3] Conformity to the image of Christ is the ultimate call of the Christian life. In order to be consciously conformed to his image, he must be our pattern and example for all of life.

The New Testament is not ambiguous in presenting our Lord Jesus as both redeemer and example. Jesus himself said, "For even the Son of Man came not to be served but to serve, and to give his life as a ransom for many" (Mark 10:45). He also said on the night of his betrayal, after washing the disciples' feet, "For I have given you an example, that you also should do just as I have done to you" (John 13:15). Peter exhorts us, "For to this you have been called, because Christ also suffered for you, leaving you an example, so that you might follow in his steps" (1 Pet. 2:21). The apostle Paul told the Corinthians, "Be imitators of me, as I am of Christ" (1 Cor. 11:1). He also instructed the Philippians, "Have this mind among yourselves, which is yours in Christ Jesus"

(Phil. 2:5). The apostle John also taught, "Whoever says he abides in him ought to walk in the same way in which he walked" (1 John 2:6).

Because Jesus is both redeemer and example, we ought to seek to follow him as such. The emotional life of our Lord forms the standard for our own emotional life. There is no better pattern by which to cultivate godly emotions than the Lord Jesus. We look to the Lord Jesus in the pages of the New Testament and take seriously his call, "Learn from me, for I am gentle and lowly in heart, and you will find rest for your souls" (Matt. 11:29). As we gaze on his beauty, we will be increasingly transformed into his image (2 Cor. 3:18).

The Devotion of Jesus

A couple in our church recently celebrated their sixty-ninth wedding anniversary. They were married in 1938. Every Sunday Bob gingerly helps Gerry into church, getting her situated and ready for worship. Gerry went through some deep waters early last summer, and we thought she was going home to be with the Lord. Bob was at the hospital every day, making sure she was receiving proper care. And she made it to their sixty-ninth anniversary. I love to listen to them talk to each other and about each other. I admire them. The word that stands out as I think of Bob and Gerry is "devotion."

Devotion communicates a deep love and an earnest commitment. There is something consuming, absorbing, and controlling about true devotion. There is no such thing as unfeeling devotion. Devotion is a word that oozes emotion. Half-hearted devotion is questionable devotion, at best, and probably not devotion at all. True devotion encompasses the feelings. It is passionate. It moves, it motivates, it inspires, and it endures.

Devotion is a word that describes our Lord Jesus Christ. In looking at our Lord's emotional life we can see that his devotion was obvious and prevalent. Our Lord was devoted to his Father, his Father's commission and commands. We could say our Lord had one holy passion: "My food is to do the will of him who sent me and to accomplish his work" (John 4:34). "I always do the things that are pleasing to him" (John 8:29).

The Lord Jesus perfectly kept his Father's commandments, even from childhood. Clifford Pond, in his delightful book *The Beauty of Jesus*, says, "The beautiful life of Jesus was one of humble and willing obedience to the will of God."[4] Christ's devotion to obedience was unwavering, passionate, and wholehearted.

Closely related to our Lord's devotion to obedience was also his devotion to submission to the Father. Jesus lived his whole life devoted to the Father's will. "I can do nothing on my own. As I hear, I judge, and my judgment is just, because I seek not my own will but the will of him who sent me" (John 5:30).

This devoted submission to the will of his Father reached its apex in the garden of Gethsemane (Luke 22:39–46). It was in that lonely place where he wrestled and prayed and sweat drops of blood. And it was in that place he stood triumphantly, determined to submit his will to the will of his Father. "Oh, rare and beautiful devotion, that can see nothing to be regarded save that will, even when it brings against Him all the pains of death and terrors of hell; even when Apollyon, with all his poisoned darts and hideous emissaries, is darkening the very sky, that can still calmly say, 'I delight to do Thy will, O my God.'"[5]

The Scriptures reveal our Savior as one who was completely devoted to obeying and submitting to his Father. Our Lord was also perfectly devoted to godly zeal. He was so devoted to the Father's glory and so zealous for his Father's name that he drove the moneychangers out of the temple. His disciples watched as coins and dove feathers flew, and charlatans ran for their lives. Their thoughts gravitated towards Scripture and its fulfillment. "Zeal for your house will consume me" (John 2:17; cf. Ps. 69:9).

Our Lord Jesus models for us what it means to be devoted to God. Many times we struggle with being devoted to the wrong things. Ask those around you, "Do you know what I am devoted to? Can you tell what I am passionate about?" Ask your kids. Ask your spouse. If the answers have to do with football teams, rock bands, or cars, and Jesus does not make the list, then something is very wrong. If we are going to cultivate the godly emotions of devotion to Christ—in obedience, submission, and zeal—then we might need to start with confession and repentance.

What will stir our devotion to Christ will be nothing less than looking to Christ, asking him to fill us with himself and his Spirit.

The Delight of Jesus

I remember the first time I saw John Piper's book *Desiring God*. The title was orthodox enough; all Christians should desire God. It was the subtitle that gave me a serious case of the hives, *Meditations of a Christian Hedonist*. I remember thinking, "There are some words that should never go together; 'Christian' and 'hedonist' are two of them!" What I did not realize was the theme of pleasure is a predominant biblical theme. The notion of delight pervades the Bible.

The concepts of delight and pleasure are concepts that fully engage the emotions. Delight without feeling would be like saying, "sweet without taste." What is amazing is that these concepts are everywhere in the Bible, no less in the life of our Lord. B. B. Warfield remarkably notes, "If our Lord was the Man of Sorrows, He was more profoundly still the Man of Joy."[6] What did our Lord delight in? He delighted to do the Father's will (Heb. 10:5–7; Isa. 11:3). There was not only a devotion to do the Father's will, but there was also a satisfaction and delight that came in doing his will. Our Lord, as the Sweet Psalmist of Israel, could say, "I delight to do Your will, O my God" (Ps. 40:8, NASB).

Our Lord delighted in communion with the Father. We find him often slipping away to have time alone with his Father. There is every reason to believe these times were marked by pleasure on Jesus' part. What David could say in Psalm 16 could find consummate fulfillment only in David's greater Son: "For you will not abandon my soul to Sheol, or let your holy one see corruption. You make known to me the path of life; in your presence there is *fullness of joy*; at your right hand are *pleasures* forevermore" (Ps. 16:10–11). "In the secret place of the Most High, He found His elixir of life, and He came forth from the presence-chamber, rejoicing like a strong man to run a race."[7]

Jesus was a man of true joy. In Luke 10:21 we read, "In that same hour he *rejoiced in the Holy Spirit* and said, 'I thank you, Father, Lord of heaven and earth, that you have hidden these things from the wise and understanding and revealed them to little children; yes, Father, for such was your gracious will.'" In Hebrews 1:9 we read of him, "You have loved righteousness and hated wickedness; therefore God, your God, has anointed you with the *oil of gladness* beyond your companions" (Heb. 1:9; cf. Ps. 45:6–7). The writer to the Hebrews also wrote that it was joy that motivated Christ in the enduring the agony of the cross (Heb. 12:2). Warfield is emphatic:

> It cannot be supposed that Jesus prosecuted His work on earth in a state of mental depression. His advent into the world was announced as "good tidings of great joy," and the tidings which He Himself proclaimed were "the good tidings," by way of eminence. It is inconceivable that He went about proclaiming them with a sad countenance. . . . Joy He had; but it was not the shallow joy of mere pagan delight in living, nor the delusive joy of a hope destined to failure; but the deep exultation of a conqueror setting captives free. This joy underlay all His sufferings and shed its light along the whole thorn-beset path which was trodden by His torn feet.[8]

The Lord Jesus Christ is the pattern for true, wholehearted devotion and the highest and deepest delights. He was not only the man of sorrows, acquainted with grief, but he was also the man of joy, acquainted with delight. Jesus took pleasure in the things that mattered most. His great delight was in communing with God. He rejoiced in doing the work of God. He was glad in the company of his brothers. His happiness came in the fulfillment of God's purpose in his life.

One of the reasons we find it so difficult to grow in Christlikeness is that we still find far too much pleasure in the wrong things. Our delights clash with God's delights. As C. S. Lewis observed years ago, "We are half-hearted creatures, fooling about with drink and sex and ambition when infinite joy is offered us, like an ignorant child who wants to go on making mud pies in a slum because he cannot imagine what is meant by the offer of a holiday at the sea. We are far too easily pleased."[9]

The Bible does tell us to enjoy life and receive it as the gift of God.[10] We are to take pleasure in the good gifts of God in this life. But are we delighting in the gifts without delighting in the Giver? "He is not only the giver but the gift itself, for whose sake all other earthly gifts exist."[11] What about our personal hierarchy of delights? Do I delight in God and the things that ultimately matter, more than the passing gifts of this life? Looking to the Lord Jesus and seeing what brought joy to his soul are a corrective to us and a rebuke to the fact that we really are "far too easily pleased."

CHAPTER 15

Jesus Our Pattern,
Part 2

Imagine living for years without a hug or even a handshake. Imagine every place you went you had to cover your mouth and announce your arrival with the words, "Unclean! Unclean!" That was the life of lepers in Jesus' day and had been since the time of Moses (Leviticus 13–14). God needed to protect the community through detailed legislation within the larger context of purity laws. He also powerfully portrayed the horror of sin. But the life of the leper was lonely. He was an outcast, living outside of the realm of human touch and compassion.

The Compassion of Jesus

As we saw in chapter 1, God is compassionate. The theme of God's compassion is a major note in the symphony of Scripture. Exodus 34:6 is a repeated refrain throughout the Old Testament, "The LORD, the LORD God, compassionate and gracious, slow to anger, and abounding in lovingkindness and truth" (NASB). When our Lord became a man, he embodied the Father's compassion. We could say he became compassion incarnate. "The emotion which we should naturally expect to find most frequently attributed to Jesus whose whole life was a mission of mercy . . . is no doubt compassion."[1]

A word study in the Old and New Testaments reveals a richness in the biblical concept of compassion. Some words are physiological words, conveying that compassion is a feeling deep inside of us.[2] Other words emphasize the showing of mercy or compassion. These words focus on compassion in action.[3] Compassion is definitely an emotion, one of tenderness and sympathy, which motivates the giving of help. This is our Lord Jesus.

Jesus was filled with compassion toward those in physical distress, whether they were blind (Matt. 20:34), lepers (Mark 1:41), hungry (Mark 8:2) or grieving over the death of a loved one (Luke 7:13; John 11:35). Jesus was deeply moved by human suffering and need. On each occasion, he demonstrated compassion. "All His healing work cost Him feeling."[4] His acts of compassion are stirring.

Consider the leper in Mark 1:40–42. This man, under the Mosaic Law, was a social outcast. He was required to announce his presence with the declaration, "Unclean! Unclean!" (Lev. 13:45). Human touch was prohibited. But this man took an enormous risk and approached Jesus. Jesus, instead of being repulsed by the leprosy, was moved with compassion (Mark 1:41). Jesus reached out his hand and *touched him*. How long had it been since this man felt the touch of another human being? With that touch came healing. This was an object lesson of redemption, and a moving demonstration of compassion in action.

Also, Jesus had some close friends, including two sisters, Mary and Martha, and their brother, Lazarus. When Lazarus became ill, Mary and Martha sent for Jesus. Jesus delayed and Lazarus died (John 11:1–16). The Son of God knew what was in store. He delayed on purpose. His plan was secure. Nevertheless, as he saw the distress of the sisters and was taken to the place where Lazarus had been buried, he wept (John 11:30–35). Jesus, the Resurrection and the Life, who was about to raise Lazarus from the dead, was so moved with compassion over their grief that he cried. "The tears which wet His cheeks when, looking upon the uncontrolled grief of Mary and her companions, He advanced, with heart swelling with indignation at the outrage of death, to the conquest of the destroyer, they were distinctly tears of sympathy."[5]

The Lord Jesus also felt and expressed compassion toward those who had deep spiritual needs. He felt compassion for those who were like sheep without a shepherd (Matt. 9:36). His compassion for the lost of Jerusalem was expressed, "O Jerusalem, Jerusalem, the city that kills the prophets and stones those who are sent to it!

How often would I have gathered your children together as a hen gathers her brood under her wings, and you would not!" (Matt. 23:37). The sovereign Savior who revealed the Father to whomever he willed (Matt. 11:27) is also the compassionate Savior who mourns the lost condition of an entire city. "It hurt Jesus to hand over even hardened sinners to their doom."[6]

The Lord Jesus is our pattern for compassion. He feels for his people in their affliction (Heb. 4:15). He promises, out of compassion, to deal gently with his sheep. He feels for those who are sick and suffering. He has compassion for the lost and perishing, even in their rebellion against his rule. The compassion of Jesus should mold and shape our own emotions. If our theology cuts the nerve of compassion for the lost then our theology is not biblical. If our theology stultifies compassion for the suffering, then we are not thinking or feeling like our Savior. We need to see people as Jesus sees them and feel for them as he feels for them.

The apostle John asks, "But if anyone has the world's goods and sees his brother in need, yet closes his heart against him, how does God's love abide in him?" (1 John 3:17). Paul exhorts us, "Put on then, as God's chosen ones, holy and beloved, compassionate hearts, kindness, humility, meekness, and patience" (Col. 3:12). Peter tells us, "Finally, all of you, have unity of mind, sympathy, brotherly love, a tender heart, and a humble mind" (1 Pet. 3:8).

May God the Father, who is full of compassion, and the Lord Jesus, who is our model of compassion, fill us through the Holy Spirit with the holy emotion of compassion that compels us to relieve suffering, misery, loneliness, and lostness wherever we can. When we do that, people will see Jesus.

The Love of Jesus

I have officiated at quite a number of weddings over the years, and I have been asked frequently to include 1 Corinthians 13, the love chapter, in the ceremony. The request is not inappropriate. The couple should look to 1 Corinthians 13:4–7 as inspired directions on how to love each other. But let us never miss the fact that the Lord Jesus personifies love as it is described in 1 Corinthians

13:4–7.[7] If you want to see love in all its emotion and expression, look to Christ. He is love incarnate.

He perfectly fulfilled the first and second great commandments, to love God with everything we are and our neighbors as ourselves (Matt. 22:34–40; cf. Deut. 6:5; Lev. 19:18). Christ loved his Father with a pure love. His whole life was absorbed with love to the Father. His love for God encompassed the whole man: heart, soul, mind, and will. Therefore, love to the Father was obedience to the Father. When his hour finally comes, with holy determination and resolution, he makes it clear that he is doing it because he loves the Father. "I will no longer talk much with you, for the ruler of this world is coming. He has no claim on me, but I do as the Father has commanded me, so that the world may know that I love the Father. Rise, let us go from here" (John 14:30–31).

Jesus also demonstrated the second great commandment, which is neighbor love. Jesus loved people who would not follow him, as in the case of the rich young ruler: "And Jesus, looking at him, loved him" (Mark 10:21). He loved his close friends (John 11:3–5). He had a special love for his disciples: "As the Father has loved me, so have I loved you. Abide in my love" (John 15:9); and "Having loved his own who were in the world, he now showed them the full extent of his love" (John 13:1, NIV). He also loved his enemies. He practiced what he preached, "But I say to you who hear, Love your enemies, do good to those who hate you, bless those who curse you, pray for those who abuse you" (Luke 6:27–28).

As our Lord was being crucified, the unspeakable pain did not distract his attention from others, including those who were causing his pain. Even his enemies, those who were abusing him and cursing him, were not outside the orbit of his love. How did Jesus love his enemies? He prayed for them. "And Jesus said, 'Father, forgive them, for they know not what they do'" (Luke 23:34). J. C. Ryle remarks, "The fruits of this wonderful prayer will never be fully seen until the day when the books are opened, and the secrets of all hearts are revealed."[8]

Quite honestly, some of these commands seem impossible to

us. We find our hearts divided and our loves tainted. We sing it. "In my heart there is a treason, one that poisons all my love."[9]

Loving our enemies? Loving others? The standard, Christ himself, makes the call to love seem insurmountable. But it is right here where we can begin to rejoice and actually feel hope. The call to love others as ourselves, love our enemies, and love God with everything in us, is not written on tablets of stone, which hang over us for our condemnation. This call is written upon our hearts (Jer. 31:31–33). This love is poured out in our hearts through the Holy Spirit (Rom. 5:5).

The love of Christ is something God puts in us as a result of saving us. "We know that we have passed out of death into life, because we love the brothers. Whoever does not love abides in death. . . . By this we know love, that he laid down his life for us, and we ought to lay down our lives for the brothers" (1 John 3:14, 16). We find the truth of implanted love very clearly here:

> Beloved, let us love one another, for love is from God, and whoever loves has been born of God and knows God. Anyone who does not love does not know God, because God is love. In this the love of God was made manifest among us, that God sent his only Son into the world, so that we might live through him. In this is love, not that we have loved God but that he loved us and sent his Son to be the propitiation for our sins. Beloved, if God so loved us, we also ought to love one another. (1 John 4:7–11)

It is God in Christ who is the author and fountain of this love. So when we feel unloving, when we struggle to love God with all that we are, or when we struggle to love others, we continue to sing, "Take my heart and consecrate it, wash it in Your cleansing blood."[10]

In order for Christlike love to be cultivated in our hearts, we must marinate in his love for us, especially his love demonstrated on the cross. We must preach to ourselves that we can love because God first loved us. We can have our hearts overflow with love for others that goes beyond anything we could ever imagine. How can love not be cultivated in us if we are swimming in Christ, "the deep sweet well of love"?

The Perfect Balance of Jesus

My former seminary professor and pastor, Jim Andrews, is a master of metaphors. His brain works in pictures. Some of those metaphors, no doubt, have inadvertently worked their way into this book. But there is a metaphor for which I want to give Jim all the credit. He used to say about folks who were unstable and easily swayed, "Man, he is like a ping-pong ball in a windstorm."

The metaphor works well in describing someone who is blown all around, up and down and side to side, no stability, no balance, and no emotional equilibrium. One of the goals of this section on cultivating godly emotions is that we develop greater emotional balance and stability. This does not mean our personalities are overhauled, but it does mean we strive for a more balanced emotional life. The truth of God's Word provides ballast for our emotions. Once again, the Lord Jesus is also the pattern for emotional balance or symmetry.[11]

> Sin destroys the harmony of the human personality so that we can say that one person is an extrovert, another is an introvert, one is sluggish, one is dynamic. Part of the work of sanctification is to correct our extremes and overcome our weaknesses. That means we are to become more like Jesus Christ.[12]

Our Lord Jesus was always perfectly balanced in his emotions. His emotions never "got the better of him." Rather, there was a beautiful symmetry and appropriateness in all his emotions and their exhibitions. A number of examples illustrate our Lord's balance. When Jesus heard of the Roman centurion's faith, "he marveled and said to those who followed him, 'Truly, I tell you, with no one in Israel have I found such faith'" (Matt. 8:10). The Greek word for *marvel* means "to wonder," "to be amazed," or "to be astonished." It is an emotional response, an engagement of the heart, to something that has happened. In this case, Jesus marveled at the faith of a Gentile.

About another occasion, when Jesus was in his hometown, we read, "And he could do no mighty work there, except that he laid his hands on a few sick people and healed them. And he marveled because of their unbelief" (Mark 6:5–6). Jesus marvels in Nazareth because of their unbelief. The emotions of astonishment and wonder capture the Lord's heart when confronted with the unbelief of his own hometown. "The rebuff so chilled His heart that the activity of His miraculous power was restrained."[13]

Here is an example of our Lord's emotional balance. He experienced positively the feeling of astonishment in response to the centurion's faith and negatively in response to the Nazareth Jews' unbelief. Such symmetry is the mark of emotional health, because the emotions are appropriately responding to certain values and evaluations.

We could point out the same balance when it came to our Lord's anger. His anger was always balanced, poised, and measured. In Mark 3:1–5 we see Jesus' anger in response to the hard-heartedness of the Pharisees when they closed their hearts to a man in need. His grief at their hardness of heart resulted in a righteous anger. The self-righteous Pharisees were abusing God's law and mistreating his sheep. Jesus' anger was the appropriate, balanced, measured response to his grief.

The cleansing of the temple is reported in John 2:13–17. In this incident, Christ's love for God and his house of worship appropriately resulted in anger when his Father's house was being prostituted for personal gain. His anger was manifested not because of a personal offense or insult, but because of righteous indignation and zeal for God's name.

> Here, with uplifted scourge, with indignation flaming in His eyes and vibrating in His voice, He drives the profane rabble of men and beasts from the precincts of God's house. He who was all friendliness, all benignity, is now all fire, fierce, rigorous, unsparing, consumed and carried away by passionate intolerance of whatever violated the honor of God and the sanctity of His worship.[14]

The sternness of Jesus is another example of his perfect balance. Some people think that speaking any sharp word is always wrong. Not a few believe that directness and firmness are signs of carnality. Not so. The Lord Jesus demonstrated a sternness and firmness when appropriate. Compassion and love incarnate knew how and when to give firm rebukes and stern warnings. This is not inconsistency; it is perfect balance between gentleness and firmness, grace and truth (John 1:14).

Jesus' responses were always fit for the occasion. "O you of little faith!" (Matt. 6:30; 8:26; 14:31; 16:8) was a word of rebuke the disciples needed to hear. Jesus was not being unduly critical or impatient; he was stirred by the smallness of their faith, and his words expressed his dissatisfaction.

He harshly rebuked Peter, "Get behind me, Satan! For you are not setting your mind on the things of God, but on the things of man" (Mark 8:33). He felt exasperation with his own disciples and their lack of faith: "And he answered them, 'O faithless generation, how long am I to be with you? How long am I to bear with you?'" (Mark 9:19). Peter should have known better. Jesus responded appropriately. The disciples should have done better. Jesus responded appropriately. Our Lord's emotions and their displays were in perfect proportion to Peter's idiocy and his disciples' ineptness.

I remember seeing this happen once in class while I was a seminary student. My professor was speaking of Christ's self-emptying from Philippians 2. He was deeply moved by the truths he was expounding. We could hear the passion in his voice. We could see the earnestness on his face. To the half-hearted there is something uncomfortable about such passion. To the lukewarm deep emotion is an indictment.

One of the students, in an effort to lighten up the moment, raised his hand and asked, "Is this going to be on the test?" The professor, one of the gentlest and humblest men I know, shot back with a volley that was nothing short of "get behind me, Satan." Some may say his rebukes were out of place, over the top; but in reality, there was an emotional symmetry that emerged. If he had laughed or merely dismissed the question, it would have betrayed his real values. Consistency with his values demanded that his emotional response be stern. So it always was with the Lord Jesus.

As we consider our Lord Jesus, we become painfully aware of our own emotional inconsistencies. Beware of chalking them up to temperaments. Personality classification may be nothing more than a covering for our lack of balance. Our emotional responses often do reflect our own lack of symmetry. We fail to marvel when we should. We fail to be astonished. We get angry over personal insult but are passive when God's name is blasphemed. Our harsh words flow when they should not. When they should, we are too timid to speak.

Our attachment to Jesus as his disciples should compel us to relish his beauty and delight in his perfection. As we look to him, our sins are revealed. We go to him as our Redeemer, who will cleanse us and forgive us. But we also go to him as the one who can transform us into his image.

The New Testament tells us, "Consider Jesus" (Heb. 3:1); "fix your eyes on Jesus" (Heb. 12:2, NIV); "behold his glory" (2 Cor. 3:18). The apostles call us to imitate Christ, walk as he walked, and follow in his steps. There are no magical formulas to becoming more like Jesus. It is a supernatural process, which requires us to behold him, to meditate upon him, and to fix the eyes of faith on him. We become like what we behold (Pss. 115:4–8; 135:15–18; 2 Cor. 3:18).

We need to fill our minds with Christ. We read of him in the Word, from Genesis to Revelation. We see him up close and personal in the Gospels. We soak in his benefits in the Epistles. We kindle our hope in him in the Revelation. We need to read Christ-centered, Christ-saturated authors who have the gift of displaying Christ in the written word.[15] We must listen to Christ preached from the Bible in our churches. We need to sing of Christ in the songs of Zion, old and new. Let the words of the Christ-besotted John Owen find a place in our hearts:

> It is by beholding the glory of Christ by faith that we are spiritually edified and built up in this world, for as we behold His glory, the life and power of faith grow strong and stronger. It is by faith that we grow to love Christ. So if we desire strong faith and powerful love, which give us rest, peace and satisfaction, we must seek them by diligently

beholding the glory of Christ by faith. In this duty I desire to live and die. On Christ's glory I would fix all my thoughts and desires, and the more I see of the glory of Christ, the more the painted beauties of this world will wither in my eyes and I will be more and more crucified to this world. It will become to me like something dead and putrid, impossible for me to enjoy.[16]

CHAPTER 16

Renewing Our Minds

My friend wears a baseball cap that has one word embossed across the front, "Think." It seems that we should not need to be told to think, but, alas, there is reality to remind us that today there is a crisis in thinking. The centrality of biblical thinking has pervaded this book. We mortify and cultivate the emotions through truth. It is the discipline of thinking God's thoughts after him that aligns our emotions. But this raises a serious problem. There is a thinking crisis within evangelicalism. If what I have said so far is true, then there is a very strong connection between our lack of biblical thinking and the emotional confusion that I dealt with briefly in the introduction.

Numerous Christian theologians and thinkers have identified the crisis, such as Harry Blamires in *The Christian Mind* (1963); John Stott in *Your Mind Matters* (1972); Earl Radmacher in *You and Your Thoughts* (1977); John Woodbridge in *Renewing Your Mind in a Secular World* (1985); Os Guiness in *Fit Bodies Fat Minds: Why Evangelicals Don't Think and What to Do About It* (1994); and James Boice in *Renewing Your Mind in a Mindless Age: Learning to Think and Act Biblically* (2001), to name a few.

The Crucial Role of Biblical Thinking

The Bible is filled with passages that deal with the mind. There is a whole host of words that denote the importance of the activity of thinking. The mind is part of our being, which perceives truth and arrives at moral judgments. The mind is the faculty of understanding and attitude. Various passages and words in the New Testament express the ways or patterns of thought and the importance of the thinking process. Such terms as *reckon, calculate, take into account, look upon, consider, reason,* and *reflect* are used with regularity and establish the crucial role of the thinking process.[1]

There are a few Scripture passages that stand out as epitomizing the crucial role of thinking. The classic text is Romans 12:2: "Do not be conformed to this world, but be transformed by the renewal of your mind [Gk. *nous*]." Earlier in Romans, we read, "Those who live according to the flesh set their minds [Gk. *phroneō*] on the things of the flesh, but those who live according to the Spirit set their minds on the things of the Spirit. For to set the mind [*phronēma*] on the flesh is death, but to set the mind on the Spirit is life and peace" (8:5–6). Paul exhorts the Philippians, "Have this mind [*phroneō*] among yourselves, which is yours in Christ Jesus" (Phil. 2:5).[2] Later in the same letter, he states so powerfully, "Finally, brothers, whatever is true, whatever is honorable, whatever is just, whatever is pure, whatever is lovely, whatever is commendable, if there is any excellence, if there is anything worthy of praise, think [*logizomai*] about these things" (Phil. 4:8). In Colossians 3:2, Paul instructs, "Set your minds [*phroneō*] on things that are above, not on things that are on earth." Another well-known admonition is 2 Corinthians 10:5, "Take every thought [*noēma*] captive to obey Christ." This brief sampling emphasizes the crucial role of proper thinking.

Those passages cause me to reflect on my early Christian life. As I mentioned previously, I was an experience junkie for a while. My relationship with the Lord was emotionally driven. How I felt about God or myself dictated my life. God weaned me off an emotionally driven Christian life through a sermon series by Earl Radmacher, "The Power of Right Thinking." It was a cup of fresh water to my soul. However, in the midst of learning about the power of biblical thinking, I put my emotions on the shelf (which was not Dr. Radmacher's fault). My theological pendulum swung too far to the other side. But even though I went from one imbalance to another, those texts and many of the books mentioned above made an impact on my Christian life.

Later I would learn and come to appreciate not only the power of thinking God's thoughts after him (thinking biblically) but also the importance of the affections or the emotions in relationship to the mind. There is a connection.

The Thinking-feeling Connection

The Bible does not neatly separate thinking from feeling, as if they were two totally different faculties. There is often overlap between thinking and feeling, the mind and the heart, reason and emotion.[3] Although there is often overlap, there is also a dynamic relationship and connection. Right thinking should produce right feelings, and right feelings produce right actions. The corollary of this is true as well.

I have already expounded or alluded to many of these truths, but notice the connections:

• Right thinking about God produces and cultivates godly emotions such as peace, joy, confidence, and hope. "You keep him in perfect peace whose mind is stayed on you, because he trusts in you" (Isa. 26:3; see also Ps. 16:8–9; Lam. 3:19–24).

• Right thinking about Christ produces and cultivates godly, Christlike emotions like joy, compassion, righteous anger, and love (see chapters 14 and 15).

• Right thinking about spiritual realities produces and cultivates spiritual life with peace, security, and comfort (Rom. 8:5–7; Phil. 4:8–9; Pss. 55:22; 94:19).

• Right thinking about ourselves and others produces the right feelings of humility (Rom. 12:3; Phil. 2:2–5).

• Right thinking about suffering and eternity produces the affection of hope (Rom. 8:18; 2 Cor. 4:16).

• Right thinking about Christ's accomplished work of redemption motivates godly emotions for holiness, such as gratitude and tenderheartedness (Rom. 6:17–18; 12:1; 2 Cor. 5:15; Eph. 4:32).

Renewing Our Minds to Cultivate Godly Emotions

Volume 7 of John Owen's classic *The Grace and Duty of Being Spiritually Minded* is a must-read in this area.[4] But here are a few practical truths that can help renew our minds and cultivate godly emotions.

Negatively, we must watch what we put into our minds. What we put into our minds can stir up ungodly emotions and desires. One of the battles we face all day, every day, is that the world and the flesh bombard us with masterful orchestration by a crafty Devil. If we allow our minds to settle on fleshly things, we will stir up fleshly emotions. If we allow our minds to fixate on the world, we will find our emotions, desires, and actions being conformed to this world. This is not a call to legalism (a manmade list of don't watch, don't listen, etc.); it is a call to recognize that what we think about and dwell on will affect our emotions and our actions. Therefore, we are to live and think cautiously (Prov. 4:23; 27:3; Rom. 13:14).

Positively, we must consciously feed our minds on God's Word and things above. Reading the Word daily, memorizing Scripture, listening to praise and worship music, and reading edifying books are all life-changing, heart- and mind-transforming disciplines. In the following chapters, we are going to look at other Christian disciplines and means of grace. The logistics of renewing our minds is not rocket science or brain surgery. Most of it is common sense.

A challenge to all of us is to take inventory of our thoughts. What do we think about? When our minds are in neutral where do they go? Owen comments, "Ordinarily voluntary thoughts are the best measure and indication of the frame of our minds."[5] We think about the things we love, and we love the things we think about (Mark 7:21–23; 1 John 2:15–17). An inventory of our thinking will help alert us to the thoughts we need to take captive (2 Cor. 10:4–5). It can also help us to strategize in the battle for the mind and emotions.

If we consciously made an effort to renew our minds through the Word and Spirit, we will find that our love for the good, the true, and the godly would increase in proportion. Elliott concludes, "With the renewal of the mind comes a new way of feeling and new reasons for feeling. A Christian world-view will ultimately transform the emotions."[6]

Chapter 17

The Emotions and Worship

I was trying to get over a bad case of the twenty-four-hour flu. But when I woke up that Sunday morning, I was still sick. I was scheduled to preach three times at a church about forty-five minutes away from my home. I went through all the unpleasant mechanics of the flu numerous times before I left, praying earnestly that each time would be the last time. I drove to the church quickly, then found the associate pastor and the bathroom. God carried me through the two morning services. I had one more to go, the evening service.

After preaching the second morning sermon, I went to the pastor's home instead of driving back to my house. I slept all afternoon. I woke up about an hour before the evening service and felt weak but a little better. The associate pastor told me that although their evening service is similar to their morning service, it is also a little different. I had no way of knowing how different.

The worship service started, and it was loud. My headache came back with a vengeance. The "worship leader" was a lounge singer from the casinos in Tahoe who knew how to work the crowd. The music got louder, the people got louder. There was very little content in the singing, but there was a whole lot of piano, guitars, and drums. People were clapping and dancing, and I was ready to look for the bathroom again. As I fought the effects of the flu, I felt disturbed. There was no substance in the worship songs. It was very, very emotional. People were happy, clapping and swaying. But was it worship?

I can imagine some of my ministerial peers shaking their heads with grief and even some disgust, saying, "Of course that was not worship; it was sheer carnality." They may be right. But this is one end of the worship spectrum. I have been in a few churches where the worship was characterized by rich theology put to minor keys that many ordinary worshipers could not sing. On this end of the spectrum the atmosphere was quiet, but that was because very few people were singing. Any expression of exuberance or joy would have been suspect. These few occasions felt more like funeral services than worship services.

Opposite ends of the spectrum: one stilted, stuffy, and reserved; the other raucous and unrestrained. Good content with no emotion versus no content with lots of emotion. Which one is worship? Could it be that both situations in a strange way suffered from the same malady, just from different directions?[1]

What we are going to look at in this chapter has nothing to do with the worship wars, i.e., traditional style versus contemporary. Such debates miss the point. There was a time when Isaac Watts's music was considered contemporary worship music. There was a time when Psalm 2 was new. The age of a song, the kinds of instruments, and the use of a projector screen or a hymnal are not the issues. I want us to explore the relationship between worship and the emotions. I want to answer the question, "Why do we sing?" Finally, I want to demonstrate that God-centered, truth-saturated worship cultivates godly emotions. Although worship is larger than singing, I want to narrow our focus on the act of singing in corporate worship.

Biblical Faith Is a Singing Faith

Our faith is a singing faith. Believers in both Testaments and throughout the ages have been singing believers. Whether the song of deliverance at the Red Sea (Exodus 15), or the Psalms,[2] or the New Testament hymns,[3] or the church triumphant in heaven (Revelation 4–5; 15), the church has always been a singing church. Wherever you go throughout the world and find Christians, you will hear singing. We are the people of the Book. But the people of the Book sing. We are people who cherish truth and in turn worship in Spirit and truth. We are people who believe in theology, but theology should move us to doxology, that is, God-glorifying worship. So why do we sing?

*We Sing Because Truth Expresses and Stirs
the Emotions*

If we were to review biblical anthropology for a minute, we might recall that we are to reflect God because we are made in his image and likeness. As the image bearers, we are thinking and feeling beings. When we sing, we do not, or at least should not, engage in mindless chants, mantras, or meaningless repetition that is void of content. As Christians, we sing truth. We sing songs that have biblical content. We sing the gospel. We sing the Scripture. We engage the mind with lofty words, ideas, and concepts about the Trinity, creation, providence, and redemption. But we are not just reading these truths; we are singing these truths.

Singing has to do with the emotions. Singing engages the emotions. Although singing is never less than the engagement of the mind, it is always more. The truth enters the mind, captures the thoughts, and then moves the heart. Singing God's praise comes from the soul filled with joy. "You have turned for me my mourning into dancing; You have loosed my sackcloth and girded me with gladness, that *my* soul[4] may sing praise to You and not be silent O Lord my God, I will give thanks to You forever" (Ps. 30:11–12, nasb). Not only are we wired to perceive God's truth with the mind, but we are also wired to have the truth move the emotions, and we manifest those emotions in song.

But there is more. Singing is not only a response of our emotions to the truth; singing is also designed to stir our heart with truth. *Singing is for both expressing and stirring.*

My friend Art Azurdia told me about an experience he had in Africa. A church leader told him, "When we are happy, we sing, and when we aren't happy, we sing until we get happy." Jonathan Edwards agrees:

> The duty of singing praises to God seems to be appointed wholly *to excite and express* religious affections. No other reason can be assigned

why we should express ourselves to God in verse rather than in prose, and do it with music, but only that such is our nature and frame that these things have a tendency to move our affections.[5]

If our minds apprehend the glorious truths of God—his majesty and greatness, the glory of his Son Jesus Christ and his person and work—then we will want to sing. To truly see and taste God in truth is to express it in song. If we begin to sing great truth and our minds are focused, then our hearts will be stirred with a large range of emotions. As we sing, we should feel reverence and awe before our awesome and holy God.[6] We should feel the emotions of love and gratitude for what God has done (see Pss. 7:17; 13:6; 90:14). At other times, we should feel contrition and remorse because of our sin (Psalm 51).

But the predominant emotion that is expressed and stirred should be joy. "I will be glad and exult in you; I will sing praise to your name, O Most High" (Ps. 9:2). It is very tempting to list all of the hymns and choruses that come to mind with each of these various emotions. How can we fail to express and excite emotion when we consider the glorious truths of the gospel and the glories of God?

We are not after empty emotionalism, stirred by musical rhythms. Nor are we after lifeless singing of profound truth. We should seek to worship God with our minds and our emotions fully engaged. We should seek to stir the emotions with truth in song and express our emotions in our singing. Jesus told us, "God is spirit, and those who worship him must worship in spirit and truth" (John 4:24).

Don Carson summarizes what it means to worship in Spirit and truth. It is "essentially God-centered, made possible by the gift of the Holy Spirit, and in personal knowledge of and conformity to God's Word-made-flesh, the one who is God's 'truth,' the faithful exposition and fulfillment of his saving purposes. The worshippers whom God seeks worship him out of the fullness of the supernatural life they enjoy ('in spirit'), and on the basis of God's incarnate Self-Expression, Christ Jesus himself."[7]

We Sing Because God Sings

Since we bear the image of God, and our emotions compel us to sing, then we might conclude that God sings too. Scripture seems to indicate that God does sing. Psalm 105:43 says something interesting about the exodus: "So he brought his people out with joy, his chosen ones with singing." It might be the people who were brought out were expressing joy and singing, and no doubt, they did. But the passage is also open to the possibility that as God brought out his people, he did it with joy and singing.

Other texts are less ambiguous. "The LORD your God is in your midst, a mighty one who will save; he will rejoice over you with gladness; he will quiet you by his love; he will exult over you with loud singing" (Zeph. 3:17). This is not just humming a tune; this is joyful, loud singing. God rejoices in and sings over his redeemed people who display his grace and power. There is something stunning about this. God is a joyful God who jubilantly sings over his grace projects.[8] If we bear his image and are to image him, how could we not jubilantly return the praise for being his grace projects?

We Sing Because of God's Greatness and Glory

The theme of God's greatness and glory pervades the Psalms. "Great is the LORD and greatly to be praised in the city of our God!" (Ps. 48:1). All of God's attributes, all of his character traits, all of his works, and his love and covenant commitment to his people are all reasons to joyfully worship him in song.

> But I will sing of your strength;
> > I will sing aloud of your steadfast love in the morning.
> For you have been to me a fortress
> > and a refuge in the day of my distress.
> O my Strength, I will sing praises to you,
> > for you, O God, are my fortress,
> > the God who shows me steadfast love. (Ps. 59:16–17)

> Oh come, let us sing to the LORD;
> > let us make a joyful noise to the rock of our salvation!

Let us come into his presence with thanksgiving;
let us make a joyful noise to him with songs of praise!
For the Lord *is a great God,*
and a great King above all gods. (Ps. 95:1–3)

We Sing Because of God's Redeeming Grace

As soon as the Israelites crossed the Red Sea, having been delivered from bondage and from Pharaoh's army, they sang (Ex. 15:1–21). They celebrated their redemption with songs of praise. The experience of redemption not only leads to singing; it also implants songs of praise in the heart. "He put a new song in my mouth, a song of praise to our God" (Ps. 40:3). When the Father draws a sinner to himself in salvation, he not only saves a sinner, he also makes a worshiper. "But the hour is coming, and is now here, when the true worshipers will worship the Father in spirit and truth, for the Father is seeking such people to worship him" (John 4:23). "But you are a chosen race, a royal priesthood, a holy nation, a people for his own possession, that you may proclaim the excellencies of him who called you out of darkness into his marvelous light" (1 Pet. 2:9). "The heart sings because it is overflowing with Christ."[9]

We Sing Because God Commands Us to Sing His Praise

The commands to sing God's praise abound in Scripture. It is true to say that God demands our praise. But this is not because God is some cosmic megalomaniac who is looking for strokes. The command to praise is a righteous command because God is the most infinitely valuable person in the whole universe, and not to praise him would be cosmic treason and a moral violation of the highest good. So the Bible is filled with commands such as, "Sing praises to the Lord, O you his saints, and give thanks to his holy name" (Ps. 30:4). "Shout for joy in the Lord, O you righteous! Praise befits the upright. Give thanks to the Lord with the lyre; make melody to him with the harp of ten strings! Sing to him a new song; play skillfully on the strings, with loud shouts" (Ps. 33:1–3).

The commands are not *mere* commands like "just do it because

I said so." There are always reasons behind the commands, for instance, his greatness, his mercy, and his holiness. So the commands to sing praise are morally good because it is morally right to praise the greatest person in the universe. The commands are buttressed with reasons for praise; namely, God's person and works. And the commands involve the emotions, how the singing of his praise should be done: loudly, joyfully, and with thanksgiving.

We Sing Because We Will Be Singing throughout Eternity

One day after service, an agitated woman approached me and said, "Why do we have to sing so much? Do you realize we sang for 25 minutes?"

I could not help myself. "You'd better get used to it or you won't enjoy heaven. Singing God's praise will be our eternal joyful employment."

Worship is the business of heaven. Angels sing God's praise. The redeemed sing God's praise. It is marvelous to consider the reality that as the church sings on earth it is joining in as the church sings in heaven. In the new heavens and the new earth, we will be singing to our great God new songs of praise throughout all eternity. God has given these snapshots to us:

And they sang a new song, saying, "Worthy are you to take the scroll and to open its seals, for you were slain, and by your blood you ransomed people for God from every tribe and language and people and nation, and you have made them a kingdom and priests to our God, and they shall reign on the earth." Then I looked, and I heard around the throne and the living creatures and the elders the voice of many angels, numbering myriads of myriads and thousands of thousands, saying with a loud voice, "Worthy is the Lamb who was slain, to receive power and wealth and wisdom and might and honor and glory and blessing!" And I heard every creature in heaven and on earth and under the earth and in the sea, and all that is in them, saying, "To him who sits on the throne and to the Lamb be blessing and honor and glory and might forever and ever!" And the four living creatures said, "Amen!" and the elders fell down and worshiped. (Rev. 5:9–14)

Then I looked, and behold, on Mount Zion stood the Lamb, and with him 144,000 who had his name and his Father's name written on their foreheads. And I heard a voice from heaven like the roar of many waters and like the sound of loud thunder. The voice I heard was like the sound of harpists playing on their harps, and they were singing a new song before the throne and before the four living creatures and before the elders. No one could learn that song except the 144,000 who had been redeemed from the earth. (Rev. 14:1–3)

Conclusion

In C. S. Lewis's *Prince Caspian* there is a wonderful exchange between Lucy and Aslan.

"Aslan," said Lucy, "You're bigger."

"That is because you are older, little one," he answered.

"Not because you are?"

"I am not. But every year you grow you will find me bigger."

Worshiping God with the mind and the heart helps us to draw closer to God and to see him as bigger. Worship always needs to be in truth. But it must always be in spirit and by the Holy Spirit. Such worship gives opportunities to express and excite our emotions toward God. Worship in song can cultivate joy, gratitude, reverence, humility, repentance, and peace. Worship in song is designed to cultivate and develop godly emotions.

Have we realized that God's calling on our lives as Christians is the calling to be wholehearted worshipers of the Father, Son, and Holy Spirit? Have we embraced singing God's praise as the means by which we can express and excite our emotions through truth? Do we think about the truths we sing? Do we engage the heart and allow ourselves to be stirred? Is our singing God's praise actually causing us to grow in godly emotions? When we sing truth, our hearts respond and are stirred. To God we then can say with Lucy, "You're bigger."

CHAPTER 18

The Emotions and Preaching

We have all sat under preaching that was theologically sound and an utter chore to listen to. We have also probably been exposed to preaching that was earnest, exciting, and filled with moving stories, and, although easy to listen to, in the end was like Chinese food—leaving us hungry within 20 minutes.

Preaching can often fall off one side of the horse or the other. All light and no heat. All heat and no light. Just as God has given us his Word to inform and move us (see chapter 2), so he has also ordained the preaching of his Word to instruct our minds and move our emotions for greater godliness. Biblical preaching must be passionate if it is to live up to its name and do its job. Passionate, biblical preaching, therefore, should be a means by which we further develop and cultivate godly emotions.

Preaching in the Bible Was Passionate Preaching

In chapter 2 I argued that God reveals himself in his Word in ways that not only instruct the mind but also move the heart. I want to extend that argument here, focusing on the fact that God's Word exhibits preaching as passionate and earnest. The reason preaching must be passionate and earnest is that its chief design is not only to inform but also to move. We begin with the preaching of the prophets.

The prophets were, by definition, preachers, and their preaching was filled with passion and imagery for the purpose of making an impression on the hearers. One of Hosea's sermons likens Yahweh to a lion who is ready to tear Judah to shreds and carry God's people away until in their affliction they seek his face (Hos. 5:15–16).

Isaiah also overflows with vivid, graphic language as he preaches the oracles of divine revelation to the people of God, appealing not only to the head but also to the emotions:

> *Ho! Every one who thirsts, come to the waters;*
> *And you who have no money come, buy and eat.*
> *Come, buy wine and milk*
> *Without money and without cost.*
> *Why do you spend money for what is not bread,*
> *And your wages for what does not satisfy?*
> *Listen carefully to Me, and eat what is good,*
> *And delight yourself in abundance.* (Isa. 55:1–2, NASB)[1]

The prophets' words of comfort and consolation also drip with emotion. As they communicate with a displaced, scattered, dispirited people, they use language that moves the heart (e.g., Jer. 32:40–41; Zeph. 3:14–17). The promises are not coldly stated in legalese. The promises of comfort come with a gripping emotional power, which would have affected the people deeply with confidence of God's love for them.

Other examples are plentiful. The prophets preached to the people, "'Sing, O barren one, who did not bear; break forth into singing and cry aloud, you who have not been in labor! For the children of the desolate one will be more than the children of her who is married,' says the LORD" (Isa. 54:1). The prophets were instructed, "Cry aloud; do not hold back; lift up your voice like a trumpet; declare to my people their transgression, to the house of Jacob their sins" (Isa. 58:1). The prophets were not dry-as-dust heralds of God's revelation. They used emotional language, preached with vigor, and often demanded an emotional response. Whether they were preaching about judgment, repentance, restoration, or comfort, they poured themselves into the proclamation with the hope that the Word would impact their hearers.

John the Baptist carried on the same tradition in the same manner. He was a voice crying in the wilderness (Luke 3:3–6). There was nothing dispassionate about John's preaching. John the Baptist was no talking head spitting out information about the coming kingdom. He was a man on a mission, filled with fearlessness and power. He exemplified Micah 3:8: "But as for me, I am filled with power, with the Spirit of the LORD, and with justice and might, to declare to Jacob his transgression and to Israel his sin." Here is a taste of John's non-seeker-sensitive preaching:

> He said therefore to the crowds that came out to be baptized by him, "You brood of vipers! Who warned you to flee from the wrath to come? Bear fruits in keeping with repentance. And do not begin to say to yourselves, 'We have Abraham as our father.' For I tell you, God is able from these stones to raise up children for Abraham. Even now the axe is laid to the root of the trees. Every tree therefore that does not bear good fruit is cut down and thrown into the fire." (Luke 3:7–9)

The Lord Jesus also preached with passion and fervor. Indeed, he was not bombastic but gentle and tender (Matt. 12:15–21). Yet he also knew what it was to lift up his voice and call thirsty sinners to himself: "On the last day of the feast, the great day, Jesus stood up and cried out, 'If anyone thirsts, let him come to me and drink'" (John 7:37). When necessary, he would use the prophetic edge, preaching the woes of judgment with scathing passion (Matt. 23:13–36).

The apostles ministered in the same way. The sermons in the book of Acts are, for the most part, expositions of the Old Testament. But they are also direct, earnest, passionate, and applicatory. Paul exemplified the spirit of apostolic preaching when he wrote to the Corinthians, "Since we have the same spirit of faith according to what has been written, 'I believed, and so I spoke,' we also believe, and so we also speak" (2 Cor. 4:13). In other words, these men had been so gripped by the truth of the gospel that they had to speak (Acts 4:20). This preaching was nothing less than opening their very hearts and hoping for the same emotional response from those who heard. "We have spoken freely to you, Corinthians; our heart is wide open. You are not restricted by us, but you are restricted in your own affections. In return (I speak as to children) widen your hearts also" (2 Cor. 6:11–13).

Whether it was the prophets or the apostles, John the Baptist or the Son of God, their preaching was marked by truth on fire. It did not matter whether the sermons were filled with notes of joy or somber notes of judgment, these men were not talking heads. They did not monotonously give out the facts in a Joe Friday manner. They communicated with passion and earnestness and expected the Word to transform the whole person.

Biblical Preaching Should Engage the Emotions

Preaching is a gift that comes in different packages. There are innumerable factors that will cause the gift of preaching to be manifested in various styles. When we talk about preaching that engages the emotions, we are not talking about a particular style, a certain volume level, or a perspiration quota. We are talking about preaching that involves authentic passion and real emotion from the heart. There is no graph to chart the emotional element, but one thing is certain: we intuitively know when it is present and when it is absent. We instinctively can tell when a man preaches what he really believes (2 Cor. 4:13) or is just saying things that people are supposed to believe.

The testimony of preaching in biblical history has demonstrated that biblical preaching was passionate. Let's listen to some voices from the past. Professor John Murray stated, "To me, preaching without passion is not preaching at all."[2] The prince of preachers, C. H. Spurgeon, told his students:

> The world also will suffer as well as the church if we are not fervent. We cannot expect a gospel devoid of earnestness to have any mighty effect upon the unconverted around us. . . . The whole outside world receives serious danger from the cold-hearted preacher. . . . If the prophet leaves his heart behind him when he professes to speak in the name of God, what can he expect but that the ungodly around him will persuade themselves that there is nothing in his message, and that his commission is a farce.[3]

Presbyterian pastor and educator Thomas Murphy wrote in his Pastoral Theology:

To preach in a cold, unfeeling manner, to preach without earnestness, is sinful. It shows in the preacher a heart that is hard. . . . Deep is the guilt of handling the Word of God in an unfeeling manner! . . . What! Speak coldly for God and for men's salvation! Can we believe that our people must be converted or condemned, and yet can we speak in a drowsy tone? In the name of God brethren, labor to awaken your hearts before you come to the pulpit. . . . Remember that they must be awakened or damned, and a sleepy preacher will hardly awaken them. . . . We should not be afraid of enthusiasm here. Enthusiasm is surely excusable when life and death and the souls of men and the glory of the Son of God are at stake.[4]

Charles Bridges, in *The Christian Ministry*, wrote, "The minister that does not manifestly put his heart into his sermon, will never put his sermon into the hearts of his people."[5] Finally, Jonathan Edwards stated:

If a minister has light without heat, and entertains his auditory with a learned discourse, without a savor of the power of godliness, or any appearance of fervency of spirit, and zeal for God, and the good of souls, he may gratify itching ears, and fill the heads of his people with empty notions, but it will not be very likely to reach their hearts and save their souls.[6]

Biblical Preaching Should Impact the Emotions

If the preacher is filled with the Spirit and gripped with the truth, he is likely to have an impact on the emotions of the listeners. Peter on the day of Pentecost preached in the power of the Spirit and this was the response: "Now when they heard this they were cut to the heart, and said to Peter and the rest of the apostles, 'Brothers, what shall we do?'" (Acts 2:37). Peter's message pierced through them with conviction and brought them to repentance. Paul's sermon in Pisidian Antioch had this result: "When the Gentiles heard this, they began rejoicing and glorifying the word of the Lord, and as many as were appointed to eternal life believed" (Acts 13:48).

Paul's preaching in Thessalonica also made an impact: "Our gospel came to you not only in word, but also in power and in the Holy Spirit and with full conviction" (1 Thess. 1:5). Paul used intelligible words of truth when he preached the gospel. The message had truth content for the mind. Acts 17:2–3 describes Paul's ministry to the Thessalonians as rational: "he reasoned [*dialegomai*] with them." He discussed and debated with them using arguments. It was a scriptural ministry. He reasoned with the Jews from the Old Testament by opening, explaining, unfolding texts, proving his points. It was a Christ-centered ministry. In addition, it was concrete, demanding a verdict from those who heard.

This was not emotional rhetoric to work the crowds; it was rational biblical exposition. But Paul could say later that when he had preached to them, it hadn't been with mere rational words about the gospel; there had been real power from the Holy Spirit, which had impacted them deeply. The truth had been preached and the emotions had been stirred.

Jonathan Edwards makes the connection between the emotions of the preacher and the listeners and the importance of an emotional impact:

> And the impressing divine things on the hearts and affections of men is evidently one great and main end for which God has ordained that His Word delivered in the holy Scriptures should be opened, applied and set home upon men in preaching. . . . God hath appointed a particular and lively application of His Word to men in the preaching of it, as a fit means to affect sinners with the importance of the things of religion, and their own misery and necessary of a remedy, and the glory and sufficiency of a remedy provided; and to stir up the pure minds of the saints, and quicken their affections, by often bringing the great things of religion to their remembrance.[7]

Elsewhere he said:

> I don't think ministers are to be blamed for raising the affections of their hearers too high, if that which they are affected with be only that which is worthy of affection, and their affections are not raised beyond a proportion to their importance. . . . I should think myself in the way of my duty to raise the affections of my hearers as high as I possibly can, provided they are affected with nothing but truth.[8]

Cultivating Godly Emotions through Preaching

If preaching fails to profit us, it may be the fault of the preacher. He may not be gripped by the truth he is preaching. He may leave his heart out of it. But preaching may also fail to instruct and move us because we are not ready for the event. *God-centered, Spirit-empowered, Christ-exalting, biblically saturated preaching is an event.* If we do not prepare mentally and spiritually for the event, we may shortchange ourselves. "God uses contemporary preaching to bring salvation to his people today, to build his church, bring in his kingdom. In short, contemporary biblical preaching is nothing less than a redemptive event."[9]

As we come to the preaching of the Word, we must come with the firm conviction that preaching is the authoritative proclamation of God's revelation in Jesus Christ in the power of the Holy Spirit. In our day of brief sermons filled with anecdotes and jokes, people are not confronted with the majesty of God mediated through his Word and Spirit. Is it any wonder that so many discount preaching as trite and irrelevant? Paul commended the Thessalonians for their attitude toward the preached Word: "We also thank God constantly for this, that when you received the word of God, which you heard from us, you accepted it not as the word of men but as what it really is, the word of God, which is at work in you believers" (1 Thess. 2:13).

We hear the contemporary cries of "Give me something practical! Give me something relevant!" We should be crying out, "We want to see Jesus! We want to meet God! Give us the bread of heaven!" In the New Testament it is the Word preached that is the means of giving birth to and growing faith (Rom. 10:14–17). The Word preached is the means of bringing people to a saving knowledge of Christ (1 Cor. 1:17–2:5). The Word preached is the means of spiritual growth and maturity (1 Pet. 1:23–2:3). Cotton Mather summed it up: "The great design and intention of the office of the Christian preacher is to restore the throne and dominion of God in the souls of men."[10] What could be more practical and relevant than the Word of God coming to us in power, putting Christ on display, and strengthening faith, hope, and love?

How can we cultivate godly emotions through preaching? First, we can prepare for the event. Prepare to meet and hear from God through the event of preaching. Jonathan Edwards's observation on preaching as an event is important:

> The main benefit obtained by preaching is by impression made upon the mind at the time, and not by an effect that arises afterwards by a remembrance of what was delivered. And though an after-remembrance of what was heard in a sermon is oftentimes very profitable; yet, for the most part, that remembrance is from an impression the words made on the heart at the time; and the memory profits, as it renews and increases that impression. A frequent inculcating the more important things of religion in preaching, has no tendency to raise out such impressions, but to increase them, and fix them deeper and deeper in the mind, as is found by experience.[11]

We should spend time in prayer, asking God to draw near as the pastor feeds the flock. We should ask God to give us a hunger for the Word. We should petition God to fill the pastor with the Holy Spirit. We should pray him full so he can preach us full. Instead of eating proverbial roast preacher for Sunday lunch, he ought to be in our earnest prayers Saturday nights and Sunday mornings. We need to receive the Word with great care (Luke 8:18). We need to receive it with humility (Isa. 66:1–2; James 1:21). We need to be discerning (Acts 17:11). We need to receive the Word with faith (Heb. 4:1–2) and with a view to faithful obedience (Heb. 4:11–13).[12] Such preparation will yield rich dividends.

As we come to the Word with this preparation and attitude, a biblically sound, faithful ministry can transform our minds and emotions with lasting effects. There are times when we hear the Word, and comfort and confidence will fill our hearts because of the finished work of Christ. Other times the Holy Spirit will pierce our hearts through with conviction. Still other times God's glory and greatness may evoke joy and gladness. Feelings of awe and fear in response to his awesome holiness may be the appropriate response. Love to God, love to other Christians, and gratitude and love for Christ are all emotions that should be cultivated through a faithful ministry of the Word. On any given Sunday, there may be a combination of these emotions. May God help us not only to cultivate godly emotions in our worship, but may he be pleased also to bless his Word to us so that godly emotions are developed through biblical preaching.

CHAPTER 19

The Emotions and Faith-building Relationships

Developing and cultivating godly emotions does not happen in a bubble; it happens in community. The Bible, with few exceptions, was written to communities of believers. The focus in the Bible is on the corporate body called the church. The church is the environment where we primarily live out our Christian faith. It is true we need to take our faith and Christian witness into the world. It is also true that we must order our families according to the Word of God. We want our Christian faith to be real in the world and at home. But it is not the biological family that has the priority in the New Testament; it is the Christian family under the headship of Christ (Mark 3:31–35; Luke 14:26–27). "So between the death of Christ and the last day it is only by a gracious anticipation of the last things that Christians are privileged to live in visible fellowship with other Christians. It is by the grace of God that a congregation is permitted to gather visibly in this world to share God's Word and sacrament."[1]

It is crucial to see the centrality of the church and the indispensability of authentic Christian relationships to help us grow in grace and cultivate godly emotions. It is interesting to note that many if not most of the destructive emotions condemned in the Bible are community-destroying emotions. Matthew Elliott notes, "The negative emotions in vice lists clearly refer to aggressive anti-social or destructive behavior."[2] Such sinful emotions as anger, wrath, malice, envy, jealousy, and hatred are directed toward others.

The corollary is also true. The godly emotions that are commanded and encouraged are community-building emotions. Elliott again notes, "The new life, new values, and new thinking lead to new emotions, emotions that are fundamentally different from people who are not a part of the new community."[3]

Camaraderie in the Fight against Unbelief

Because we cannot divorce our emotions from our faith, to build up our faith is also to develop and cultivate godly emotions. Two passages underscore the vital importance of being in community to build faith and love. The first is Hebrews 3:12–13, "Take care, brothers, lest there be in any of you an evil, unbelieving heart, leading you to fall away from the living God. But exhort one another every day, as long as it is called 'today,' that none of you may be hardened by the deceitfulness of sin." The danger is clear: none of us is immune from having an evil heart of unbelief. We must not overlook the connection between feeling and faith in the sin of unbelief.

> All the sinful states of our hearts are owing to unbelief in God's super-abounding willingness and ability to work for us in every situation of life so that everything turns out for our good. Anxiety, misplaced shame, indifference, regret, covetousness, envy, lust, bitterness, impatience, despondency, pride—these are all sprouts from the root of unbelief in the promises of God.[4]

The result of an unbelieving heart is deadly. It falls away from the living God. As a pastor, I have seen this too many times. The apostasy is not usually an intellectual falling away. The emotions become entangled with wrong thoughts about God. Again, wrong feelings come gushing out of wrong thinking. This is what happened at Kadesh-Barnea when the people heard the evil report from ten of the twelve spies. Fear gripped them and squashed their faith (Numbers 13–14; Heb. 3:12–4:2). Unbelief can become a vicious whirlpool that sucks the life out of our confidence in God and spins us emotionally out of control, and then our faith turns to unbelief. This is a serious warning.

The antidote to unbelief requires community: "But exhort *one another* every day." William Lane writes, "The reflexive pronoun 'one another,' which is used here instead of the reciprocal pronoun 'each other' emphasizes the mutual responsibility that each member of the community should feel for the others. The urgency for encouragement and reproof is that the community of faith experiences an unresolved tension between peril and promise."[5] This exhortation is the antidote to unbelief because it helps prevent us from being hardened by the deceitfulness of sin.

The deceitfulness of sin is both mental and emotional, beckoning us to find our happiness outside of God. We need that exposed. We need to be warned, loved, encouraged, and stirred to zeal. We need each other to fight the fight of faith and perseverance. John Piper rightly says, "The perseverance of the saints is a community project." Dietrich Bonhoeffer's words are compelling:

> God has willed that we should seek and find His living Word in the witness of a brother, in the mouth of man. Therefore, the Christian needs another Christian who speaks God's Word to him. He needs him again and again when he becomes uncertain and discouraged, for by himself he cannot help himself without belying the truth. He needs his brother man as a bearer and proclaimer of the divine word of salvation.[6]

If we are to grow in faith, fight unbelief, and cultivate godly emotions associated with our faith, then we need each other. Although it is important to be alone with God, it is also vitally important to pursue honest, authentic Christian relationships, which can mutually build faith. If we are alone, we are in danger of being slowly dragged down and eventually away with ungodly feelings and unbelieving thoughts. It is in the context of Christian community that we can be encouraged and exhorted and have our faith and emotions properly stirred afresh and strengthened.

This is more strongly buttressed later in the same epistle: "Let us consider how to stir up one another to love and good works, not neglecting to meet together, as is the habit of some, but encouraging one another, and all the more as you see the Day drawing near" (Heb. 10:24–25). Notice briefly that there is the stirring of godly emotions, in this case love. The stirring also produces good works. Assembly is required. To neglect the assembly is to endanger ourselves. As believers, we must have as one of our fundamental priorities meeting with other believers for intentional faith-building, heart-stirring, joy-producing spiritual growth and endurance.[7]

Cultivating Community-building Emotions

Godly emotions are crucial in our walk with God and each other. Again, it is within a community of believers that those emotions can be exposed and cultivated. Since our emotions reflect our values and evaluations and influence our motives and conduct, they are exposed in the "one another" environment of the church. This exposure may be an exposure of weakness or strength.

In the body of believers, we live out the "one anothers" of Scripture. If our emotions are not properly aligned with biblical truth, our instinct will be to retreat from the "one anothers." But if we *believe God enough* and *dare* to enter into the "one another" environment, our weaknesses will be exposed, and it is at that point we begin to grow. It takes desire and vulnerability before others to grow.

All of the "one another" commands demand community. Most of the "one another" commands also require emotional involvement. The New Testament commands us to love each other. This can be done only in community. "A new commandment I give to you, that you love one another: just as I have loved you, you also are to love one another. By this all people will know that you are my disciples, if you have love for one another" (John 13:34–35; see also John 15:12, 17; Rom. 12:10a; 13:8; 1 Thess. 3:12; 4:9; 1 Pet. 1:22; 1 John 3:11, 23; 4:7, 11–12).

As we seek to love others from the heart, with brotherly affection, our values are exposed. Our real loves are laid bare. If we are committed to grow in holy conduct and emotions, we will be open to the Holy Spirit's showing our weaknesses, and we will eagerly seek to learn to love.

In the authentic fellowship of believers we seek to "outdo one another in showing honor" (Rom. 12:10b); "rejoice with those who rejoice, weep with those who weep" (Rom. 12:15); "associate with the lowly. Never be wise in your own sight" (Rom. 12:16); and give care to all the members (1 Cor. 12:22–25). We are instructed, "Through love serve one another" (Gal. 5:13), and we are to do so "with all humility and gentleness, with patience, bearing with one another in love" (Eph. 4:2). And "be kind to one another, tenderhearted, forgiving one another, as God in Christ forgave you" (Eph. 4:32). The Spirit's presence and reality will result in "submitting to one another out of reverence for Christ" (Eph. 5:21); and "if one has a complaint against another, forgiving each other; as the Lord has forgiven you, so you also must forgive" (Col. 3:13). Entering into the lives of others like this and allowing others to enter our lives on the same terms requires an emotional involvement and vulnerability.

We are also required to "*encourage* one another and build one another up, just as you are doing" (1 Thess. 5:11); "*admonish* the idle, *encourage* the fainthearted, *help* the weak, *be patient* with them all" (1 Thess. 5:14); "*confess* your sins to one another and *pray* for one another" (James 5:16); and "*clothe* yourselves, all of you, with humility toward one another, for 'God opposes the proud but gives grace to the humble'" (1 Pet. 5:5). Nothing will strip back our real values like these "one another" commands. Authentic fellowship exposes selfishness, pride, bitterness, self-preservation, upside-down priorities, cowardliness, unbelief, and emotional detachment.

Real Christian fellowship not only exposes our emotional shortcomings, but also genuine expressions of godly emotions are expressed and cultivated in Christian fellowship. When believers are willing to live out the "one anothers," there is a powerful cultivation of godly emotions. When we actually dare to be sinners among sinners something amazing happens.[8] When we get serious about wanting to encourage each other, pray for each other, and walk with each other, the Holy Spirit waters our hearts with his power, and his fruit grows. When we consciously say, "We work with you for your joy" (2 Cor. 1:24) and "I will remain and continue with you all, for your progress and joy in the faith" (Phil. 1:25), there can be an explosion of mutual emotional growth in godliness.

I thank God that our church body is seeing and experiencing this in increasing measure. There is something beautiful and compelling about forsaking the "fellowship of the pious" for the "fellowship of sinners." When we begin to be honest and open with each other and to pray for and encourage one another, there is an unleashing of spiritual power and growth. The church can become a greenhouse for the cultivation and development of holy emotions. As we labor for each other's joy and faith, there is cross-pollination, and we stimulate godly emotions in each other. When this happens, it fuels faith and motivates endurance.

Bryan Jeffery Leech has captured this dynamic in his hymn "We Are God's People."

> We are a temple, the Spirit's dwelling place,
> Formed in great weakness, a cup to hold God's grace;
> We die alone, for on its own each member loses fire:
> Yet joined in one the flame burns on
> To give warmth and light, and to inspire.[9]

I conclude this chapter with a hearty "amen" to Matthew Elliott's observation:

> In an era of churches focusing on professional stage presentations and great music, perhaps, some of our churches need to revive the potluck dinner, family night and the church picnic. The church family has the most wonderful reasons to rejoice and joy and laughter should characterize our fellowship together. We are called to enjoy one another's company just as Jesus made best friends. It is only in loving and enjoying one another up close that we will be prepared to bear one another's burdens when the pain and crises of this world come rushing down upon us.[10]

CHAPTER 20

The Emotions and the Word and Prayer

I was raised in the Catholic Church. We were devout. In the late '70s, my mother came to Christ. She was the first. The "method" was simple. She was in a Christian bookstore with her sister where she picked up a Bible and randomly turned to Leviticus. Yes, Leviticus. She read some dietary laws, and the Holy Spirit put some sugar on it, and he hooked her. She started reading the Bible and came to a saving knowledge of Jesus Christ.

My dad came later. The "method" was simple. He was a truck driver for UPS and was listening to J. Vernon McGee teach through the Bible. He started bringing a Bible with him to read on his lunch hour. He came to know Christ.

I was the holdout. I was an altar boy and a very proud son of Rome. Then I started reading the Bible. The Bible shook my world to its foundation. My mom recommended I start reading in Matthew. Matthew 5:20 was a 10.0 on my personal Richter scale. "For I tell you, unless your righteousness exceeds that of the scribes and Pharisees, you will never enter the kingdom of heaven." I was sunk, and I knew it. Then God opened my eyes to see Jesus as my only hope.

The "method" was simple. I read the Bible. After I was born again, nobody told me, "You'd better read your Bible every day." It was intuitive. God's Word was my life. I could no more live without reading my Bible than I could live without eating. The Bible is not only the instrument for new life (1 Pet. 1:23; James 1:18), but it is our life (Deut. 32:47; Matt. 4:4).

195

The Word and Fullness of Joy

The thesis of this chapter is that a consistent life in the spiritual disciplines of Bible reading and prayer will generally cultivate joy and other godly emotions. This thesis rests on many truths. I want to look at two. The first is the general observation about the nature of God's Word, which we have already seen in chapters 2 and 18. Tremper Longman's comment reiterates a point I have labored to make:

> The Bible is a book that feeds our intellect, but it does far, far more than that. It arouses our emotions, stimulates our imagination, and appeals to our will. The Bible addresses us as whole people, and that is why we must come to it with our hearts—in order to experience it.[1]

The Bible was given to us to teach us, move us, and transform us. John Piper calls Scripture "kindling for Christian hedonism."[2]

The second truth this thesis rests on is the words of our Lord Jesus in John 15:11: "These things I have spoken to you, that my joy may be in you, and that your joy may be full." The Lord Jesus had spoken many things to his disciples. He was giving them his final discourse before his death (John 13–17). He had given them the model of service, predicted his betrayal, and commanded them to love one another (John 13). He comforted them with some important words about prayer, obedience, and the coming of the Holy Spirit (John 14). He then challenged them to abide in him and bear fruit (John 15). There would be more to come. After he gave them the vine and branch metaphor, he told them he had given them his Word and that his joy would be in them and their joy would be full.

What is Jesus' joy? It must be the joy of obeying and glorifying the Father and fulfilling his will. As Christ himself abides in us, his Word abides in us. As his Word abides in us, it keeps us focused on loving and living for Christ. The fullness of joy Jesus promised had to be his joy because there could be no greater joy than that. He does not offer his disciples seconds or hand-me-downs. He offers us the highest joy of abiding in him. This joy, he says, is mediated through his Word. He gave us his Word so that we could experience true joy.

The Bible puts the Father, Son, and Holy Spirit on display so that we have joyful confidence and faith in God. The Bible is our major source of joy in him (Jer. 15:16; Job 23:12; Pss. 19:8; 119:103). It revives our hearts so that we can rejoice in God (Ps. 119:25, 50, 93, 154). The Word comforts us in affliction (Ps. 119:76). It provides sustenance and hope in despair (Ps. 119:116). The Word brings strength in grief (Ps. 119:28). It brings conviction for sin (Ps. 119:176). The Word also produces awe and godly fear (Ps. 119:38, 120, 161; Isa. 66:2). It also gives us God's promises so we can rejoice in hope (Ps. 119:140; Jer. 29:10–11; Rom. 15:4; Heb. 6:13–20; 2 Pet. 1:4). "Nothing sustains hope like a serious and sustained study of the Scriptures."[3]

In the next chapter we will talk more about reading, but for now, it is enough to conclude that the Bible gives us the foundation of faith and the fountain of joy and godly emotions. The truth of God's Word shapes our beliefs and our values, and those in turn direct our emotions.

Prayer and Fullness of Joy

Jesus gave us his Word so that his joy would be in us and our joy would be full (John 15:11). He also gave us prayer in his name so that our joy would be full: "Until now you have asked nothing in my name. Ask, and you will receive, that your joy may be full" (John 16:24). Remember the thesis of this chapter: a consistent life in the spiritual disciplines of Bible reading and prayer will generally cultivate joy and other godly emotions. *Prayer cultivates joy*. This truth also comes straight from the words of Jesus.

The qualification is we need to pray in Jesus' name. "In Jesus' name," is not some magical formula we throw on the end of our prayers. It is a profound theological statement, which marks the beginning of the new era in the history of redemption. To pray in Jesus' name is to consciously approach the Father through the only Mediator between God and man (1 Tim. 2:15). It is to embrace the only access we have to God, which is in and through the Lord

Jesus Christ and our union with him (Eph. 2:18). When we pray in Jesus' name, we are saying, "Father, I have no right to come to you or be in your presence. I am unworthy. But because of your Son, his work on my behalf, and my union with him by faith, I gladly and boldly come to you."

When we come to the Father in Jesus' name, the promise is that we will receive what we ask. This is not carte blanche! This is not a proof-text for naming it and claiming it. Other qualifiers led up to this phenomenal promise. This promise comes in the context of walking in the obedience of faith and abiding in his love and his Word, with a focus on fruit-bearing for the glory of God (John 15:7–8, 16; 14:13). "Petition without devotion, seeking gifts from God though you are not living for God, will always be by-path praying."[4]

When the qualifications are met, the promise stands. God answers our prayers that flow out of a heart filled with his Word and desiring his glory. Perhaps the greatest thing about this promise of prayer is that it brings us fullness of joy. The joy of this kind of prayer is double joy. When our hearts are fixed on fruit-bearing for God's glory and he answers our prayers, then he is glorified. There is nothing that makes the God-intoxicated follower of Jesus happier than seeing his Father glorified.

The joy has another side. When we pray like this, there is a communion with God in Christ. John Owen describes the connection between prayer and the emotions: "One principal end of it [prayer] is to excite, stir up, and draw forth, the principle of grace, of faith and love in the heart, unto a due exercise in holy thoughts of God and spiritual things, with affections suitable unto them. Those who design not this end in prayer know not at all what it is to pray."[5]

As we pray to the Father through the Son in the Holy Spirit, there is communion that brings us true joy. There may be other emotions fanned into flame as we pray and are aware of God's presence. We should be filled with awe over his majesty. We should be filled with reverent fear because of his holiness. But for the Christian who is utterly confident in his union with Jesus, there will also be joy and boldness (Heb. 4:16; 10:19–22). Awe and fear experienced apart from Christ drives us away in shame. Awe and fear experienced in Christ fills us with joy, knowing that we have a blood-bought right to approach our Father through his Son. We tremble with unspeakable joy knowing we are not only safe in the Father's presence because of Christ but also welcomed into the Father's presence because of Christ.

> There is a place where Jesus sheds the oil of gladness on our heads, a place than all besides more sweet; it is the blood-stained mercy seat.[6]

Prayer reflects our values and beliefs, but it should also be shaping our values and beliefs. As we enter into the place of secret prayer we are not only pouring out our hearts; our hearts are being shaped by God-centered goals and Christ-exalting values. The Holy Spirit takes those moments to cultivate more godly emotions in us. Prayer expresses, excites, and increases godly emotions.

Revived Joy in Retirement

As I mentioned at the beginning of this chapter, my parents came to Christ before I did. They were involved in a local church for many years but then they hit a "dry spell." The drought lasted quite a while. We would talk about the Lord, and they always knew what they needed to do, but as is often the case, the desires were too weak to motivate action. Many health issues arose. My dad's retirement finally came. For his retirement party I bought him a book about one of his favorite basketball players. I had just about given up buying any more books for their souls. Then their anniversary came. My wife and I bought them a devotional book for couples. I, cynic that I am, thought to myself, "Well, this will sit on the shelf and collect dust."

One morning the phone rang. It was my dad. "Hey, your mom and I have been reading that book you bought us for our anniversary. We really like it. They have some pretty important things to say." A few days later, the phone rang again. "Brian, you need to know the Lord is really at work in our lives. We are not only reading the devotional, but we are praying together. Mom wants us to start reading the Bible together too." A few days later my mom called, "We are really enjoying reading God's Word and the book. God is really doing something in us. We are going to church this Sunday."

My parents have been revived. Their joy in the Lord has returned. They would both admit they have a long way to go, but every morning they read the Word and pray. It's simple. Nothing profound. They made their way back to the foundation and fountain through the sweet grace of our heavenly Father. They have rediscovered not only the reviving power of the Word but also the emotional realigning power of the Word and prayer. Jesus has given us his Word and prayer for the fullness of joy in him.[7]

CHAPTER 21

The Emotions and Reading, Meditation, and Imagination

God gave us a book as his self-revelation, not a major motion picture.[1] This by default means that God expects us to read. Sometimes men in our church come to me, usually after a counseling appointment or sermon in which I pointed out a book, and say, "I don't really like to read." My response is always the same. "Get over it. God expects you to read or he would not have given us a book!"

God Expects Us to Read

Reading is powerful. Revolutions have started from reading. The Reformation didn't just promote reading; reading started and fueled it. When oppressors and tyrants want to squash freedom they burn books, with authors of the books soon to follow. There is something almost mystical about a book. There is something wondrous about reading.

Years ago, I read an essay by southern Presbyterian theologian R. L. Dabney called "Dangerous Reading."[2] Dabney made a point in the essay that caught my attention. He argued that habitual reading of fiction, which arouses emotions such as sympathy, ends up dulling, even deadening, our ability to truly feel. The reason is that the feelings that are aroused are detached from reality. He went on to argue that such emotional engagement needs the grounding of reality if it is to be useful for our mental development and character.

Without defending Dabney's condemnation of fiction,[3] it is nevertheless interesting to note that if the engagement of the emotions detached from reality can deaden us, then the corollary must be true. There can be good, healthy reading that engages the feelings, is rooted in truth and reality, and helps develop our minds, character, and emotions. Reading, therefore, can be a discipline that helps cultivate godly emotions. This kind of reading focuses on content and utilizes both meditation and imagination. To cultivate godly emotions we must read our Bibles and good Christian books, especially biographies, with our hearts and imaginations.[4] The result will be a stirring of our hearts and spiritual growth and maybe even greater missionary effort and revival.

The Case for Christian Biography

It is important that Christians read not only their Bibles but also good Christian books. I am an advocate of regularly reading Christian biography. As a new Christian, I could not get enough of D. L. Moody, Charles Spurgeon, Jim Elliot, Adoniram Judson, John Calvin, George Whitefield, Jonathan Edwards, and others. Later, when I was exposed to John Piper's ministry through his annual pastors' conference, I finally connected the dots on why Christian biography has played such a major role in my own walk.

There is, first, a biblical basis for reading Christian biography. The Bible is pro-biography. Hebrews 11 is a collection of short biographies designed to motivate faith and endurance. Hebrews 12:1–2 reminds us of the "great cloud of witnesses" who surround us while we run the race. Each one of those witnesses lived a life worthy of emulation and now they serve as motivation. Hebrews 13:7 states, "Remember your leaders, those who spoke to you the word of God. Consider the outcome of their way of life, and imitate their faith." That is the purpose of Christian biography. John Piper wrote, "Christian biography is the means by which the body life of the church cuts across the centuries."[5]

The Bible not only contains biography—inspired biography, if you will—but it also exhorts us to study the works of God (Ps. 77:11–12). The works of God are displayed not only in the glories of creation, but in the lives of his people. The men and women whose lives have been recorded for us in biography are the works of God's hands. Though they are dead, they still speak, challenge, teach, and inspire. They grip and move us through their devotion to Christ, their sufferings, labors, and courage. A whole host of Christian men and women has much to teach us. I can testify that my own Christian walk is enriched when I am engaged in reading a Christian biography.[6]

Meditation and Imagination

There is a persistent call in the Scriptures to meditate on God's Word and works. Some of those calls in Scripture are among the first we memorize in our Christian life.

> This Book of the Law shall not depart from your mouth, but you shall meditate on it day and night, so that you may be careful to do according to all that is written in it. For then you will make your way prosperous, and then you will have good success. (Josh. 1:8)

> *Blessed is the man*
>> *who walks not in the counsel of the wicked,*
> *nor stands in the way of sinners,*
>> *nor sits in the seat of scoffers;*
> *but his delight is in the law of the* Lord,
>> *and on his law he meditates day and night. (Ps. 1:1–2)*

The idea behind "meditates" is contemplative reflection and thoughtful study. Muttering or reciting is also included in the concept. Biblical meditation is far from the Eastern notion of the art of emptying self. Biblical meditation is filling up the mind with truth, turning it over, thinking it through, reciting it, and reflecting upon it, focusing on God's works as well as his words. "I will remember the deeds of the Lord; yes, I will remember your wonders of old. I will ponder all your work, and meditate on your mighty deeds" (Ps. 77:11–12).

This is not particularly hard for me. As I write, I can look out my back door at the Sierra Nevada mountain range. The snow has dusted the mountaintops early this year. The blue sky is the background. Job's Peak is to the southwest. As I recover from back surgery I go for walks. As I head down our cul-de-sac and see that majestic sight, I repeat aloud, "I lift up my eyes to the hills. From where does my help come? My help comes from the LORD, who made heaven and earth" (Ps. 121:1–2). I ponder the reality that my Father made those mountains, and it was easy for him. I ponder their bigness and my smallness and marvel that the One who made them is for me (Rom. 8:31). Each walk ends with praise because of ponder.

Part of meditation and reflection is the use of the imagination. I am not talking about child's play. I am referring to the God-given ability to think in images and create scenes in our minds. A sanctified use of our imagination brings color and vividness to our meditations. We touched on this in chapter 2 when we looked at the nature of the written Word. The extension of saying that God has spoken to us, not only to inform us but also to move us, is to say he wants us to engage with his Word emotionally and experientially. We do that through the imagination. Longman has noted in his wonderfully titled book *Reading the Bible with Heart and Mind*:

> The Bible speaks to the whole person. Its stories seize our imaginations. Its poems pluck our heartstrings. The events and images do more than simply inform us; they suck us into the "story" of our God, bring us into His life. And none of this will let go of us until we are changed people.[7]

The Connection between Meditation and the Emotions

In Psalm 39 David was frustrated with some life circumstance unknown to us. He wanted to walk carefully, not sinning with his tongue. He said he kept his frustration bottled up. He pondered the issue, he mused, he turned it over and over, and this was the result: "My heart became hot within me. As I mused, the fire burned" (Ps. 39:3). The distressing circumstance is not our focus. Rather, the focus is the fire that burned when David mused, pondered, and meditated.

There is a direct connection between meditation and a burning in our hearts—an emotional stirring. That connection may be negative, dwelling on a hurt or a disappointment and then being fired up with anger or bitterness. But the connection can also be positive, dwelling on truth, God, his Word, his works, and getting fired up with holy emotions. As we meditate, the fire burns.

Reading the Bible and Biography with Meditative Imagination

Keep in mind that the frequently played note in this book is that God's Word comes to us to inform us intellectually and also to shape and stir us emotionally. This is why God uses narrative (story), poetry, and vivid imagery.[8] When we read the Bible, we need to enter prayerfully into the story. We need to use sanctified imagination, "not going beyond what is written" (1 Cor. 4:6). When we read Christian biography, we need to transport ourselves in time, remembering the reality of the events and reliving them as we read. In my book on preaching, I note:

> While reading the narratives of the Scripture or the riveting events of Christian biography, the man of God should exercise a sanctified imagination, placing himself within earshot of the groans of Gethsemane, the weeping of the overwhelmed Joseph, the sobs of a grief-stricken David after losing Absalom, and the cry of dereliction from the Mighty Sufferer of Calvary. The imagination can transport the man of God to the hall at Worms, where Christ-centered courage and Biblical reformation won the day. The imagination needs to hear the words above the flames at the stakes at Oxford, "Be of good comfort, Master Ridley, and play the man; we shall this day light such a candle by God's grace, in England, as I trust shall never be put out." The waves covering the heads of the two Margarets at Solway Firth, or the heads of Covenanters on the Netherbow, should grip the imagination. The mind should move the heart as the five missionaries sang, "We Rest on Thee" the morning of their martyrdom on the beach of the Curaray River. These are real events and the imagination should lock into the reality of them; playing them in the theater of the mind. The use of the imagination in this way cultivates the emotions and their proper expression.[9]

Sometimes reading aloud can help us to focus on a biblical passage or biography and bring it to life. The impact of reading with meditation and imagination is often incalculable. Engaging the heart while we read Scripture can draw us in and change us. Spending time going over the words, rehearsing the scenes, and hearing the words can cause our hearts to burn with holy emotions (Luke 24:32). I wonder how many have heard the call to serve Christ among the nations because of David Brainerd's or Jim Elliot's biographies. Incalculable indeed!

Conclusion

With Jesus Christ as our perfect model, we can rely on the Spirit and the Word to transform us into his image. Our prayer should reflect the old spiritual: "Lord, I want to be like Jesus in my heart." This requires the cultivation of godly emotions. Our Father has provided for us all we need for the cultivation process: the Word, prayer, worship, biblical preaching, Christian relationships, the church present and past, and good books. As we use our Father's provisions with their proper designs, we will find our godly emotions growing to God's glory.

Wrapping It Up

For some reason, many evangelicals have become suspicious of the emotions and generally discount them. This is tragic. Others have so exalted experience and the emotions that they have minimized truth, doctrine, and theology. This too is tragic. The glorious reality is that truth and emotions, faith and feelings, theology and experience are not enemies, but the best of friends. If we discount the emotions for the so-called sake of the mind and truth, we end up missing a very big part of what we are as image bearers. We also force ourselves to misinterpret a multitude of passages that command our feelings. If we diminish the importance of the emotions we are not only denying a fundamental part of our humanity, we are also robbing God of a part of us that needs to be sanctified for his glory.

Robust, God-centered, Christ-exalting theology is designed by its Author to cause us to worship him with joy and gladness. Theology is not an end in itself. Worship is. The feeling, sovereign

God of the Bible has revealed his glory to us in his Word so we would not simply know him and think his thoughts after him, but also feel his feelings after him.

Our emotions reflect what we truly believe and what is at the very core of our being. As Christians, redeemed by the triune God, we have a relationship with him and have the privilege of being his people, living in community, and we have an eternal inheritance; our emotions should intensify as those realities grip us more deeply. As Mark Talbot said, "Our emotions betray our spiritual state." Therefore, part of our calling in the life of faith is to deal with our feelings. We need to root out the negative emotional expressions that the Bible identifies as sinful, and we need to cultivate those godly emotions that the Word commands and Jesus exemplifies. Sinful emotional manifestations can be put to death, and godly emotions can be developed and cultivated.

Postscript

I am a pastor who loves theology. I am thankful to God that in his kind providence he directed me to such teachers as John Piper, Jonathan Edwards, John Owen, J. I. Packer, and Martyn Lloyd-Jones, to name a few, who have been used by God to weld together truth and passion, doctrine and devotion, theology and doxology, and faith and feelings in my heart. This has shaped my ministry. I believe that God has used the welding together of these realities to produce a healthy (not perfect) church. I don't know why our theological stream has diluted what our forefathers seemed to see clearly, but may God restore to us the beauty of our emotions to his intense praise and enjoyment!

Divine Impassibility: Is God Really without Passions?

The early Christian apologists had their hands full. First, they were considered atheists because they denied the pantheon of Greek and Roman gods. Second, they lived in a culture where the concepts of deity were nothing more then "humanified" gods. The gods of the age were petty, hot-tempered, lustful, moody, and mischievous. The God of the Bible, on the other hand, is majestic, infinite, glorious, and transcendent. Such a view of God was difficult for the pagan mind to grasp.

In order to widen the gap between the dismal views of deity present in a pagan Roman culture and the transcendent God of the Bible, the apologists asserted that God was impassible, that is, without emotions, feelings, or passions. He didn't throw fits; he wasn't capricious or moody. In fact, he was without emotions or feelings. This made eminent sense when it was seen that God is immutable. How could variable, fluctuating, and flawed passions exist within the perfect deity of Holy Scripture? They could not. What was philosophically asserted by the apologists made its way into the Christian theological tradition.

Bruce Ware, in his excellent work *God's Greater Glory*, shows the concern was twofold. It was metaphysical and moral. In metaphysical terms, if God is immutable and eternal, then he cannot experience variations in his emotional states. In moral terms, to assert that God had emotions opened him up to moral weakness, vulnerability, and excess. The gods of the day were given to temper tantrums, mood swings, moral flaws and weakness, and an unpredictable mutability. That was definitely not the God of the Bible.

Divine impassibility was designed to protect the immutability, eternality, and moral character of God.

For some reason the philosophical assertion and theological deduction of impassibility made its way down through the centuries, even into the Reformed Confessions. In the classic language of the Westminster Confession of Faith, God is "without body, parts, or passions" (2.1). Although many theologians qualified the term "without passions," the idea that God did not have emotions still carried theological weight.

But what do we do with hundreds of texts that deal with God's emotions? Bruce Ware sums up the concern, saying, "While upholding the full transcendence of God in every way that Scripture demands, we should not conceive of God's transcendence so that other clear teachings of Scripture have to be eliminated—as I fear some have with Scripture's teaching about God's emotions."[1] Don Carson points out that when we simply reduce God's emotions to anthropopathisms,[2] "the price is too heavy. You may then rest in God's sovereignty, but you can no longer rejoice in His love. You may rejoice in a linguistic expression that is an accommodation of some reality of which we cannot conceive, couched in the anthropopathism of love. Give me a break."[3] The great Princetonian theologian Charles Hodge makes a similar point:

> The schoolmen, and often the philosophical theologians, tell us that there is no feeling in God. This, they say, would imply passivity, or susceptibility of impression from without, which it is assumed is incompatible with the nature of God. Here again we have to choose between a mere philosophical speculation and the clear teaching of the Bible, and of our own moral and religious nature. Love of necessity involves feeling, and if there be no feeling in God, there can be no love.[4]

Let me reiterate what was said about God's emotions in chapter 1. We must keep in mind that God's emotional capacities are both invulnerable and perfect. His emotions are not dependent on anything outside of himself. Although he responds and is moved by human events, he is never emotionally vulnerable, never surprised by an event or overcome with emotion. His feelings are not subject to sinfulness, since he is holy. His emotions are perfectly righteous in their essence and display. His emotions are also in perfect harmony with all his other attributes.[5]

When we come to our Bibles we should be convinced that the God of the Bible is indeed unchanging in his nature and ethics (Mal. 3:6; James 1:17). But we should also be easily convinced that he freely enters into time and space and relationships with his creatures and has emotions that are perfect, invulnerable, holy, and appropriate. That is what obviously separates God's emotions from ours. J. I. Packer notes:

> God has no passions—this does not mean that He is unfeeling (impassive), or that there is nothing in Him that corresponds to emotions and affections in us, but that whereas human passions—especially the painful ones, fear, grief, regret, despair—are in a sense passive and involuntary, being called forth and constrained by circumstances not under our control, the corresponding attitudes in God have the nature of deliberate, voluntary choices, and therefore are not of the same order as human passions at all.[6]

Is there a sense in which we can say that God is impassible? Frankly, I would rather toss the term. But Robert Reymond's comments are worth noting:

> Whenever divine impassibility is interpreted to mean that God is impervious to human pain or incapable of empathizing with human grief it must be roundly denounced and rejected. When the Confession of Faith declares that God is "without . . . passions" it should be understood to mean that God has no bodily passions such as hunger or the human drive for sexual fulfillment.[7]

We must take into account all of Scripture and allow Scripture to interpret Scripture. When it comes to attributing body parts to God (e.g., eyes, arm, hand, etc.) we note that God is spirit, and omnipresent and immense. We interpret Scripture with Scripture and properly conclude that God's "hand" is a metaphor for his power, and so on. But when it comes to declarations about his emotions, that is not necessary. We are not taking anything away from his essential and ethical immutability or his moral perfections when we assert that he has perfect emotions.[8] In fact, our view of God becomes all the more glorious when we see his perfect emotions, and then we realize that we are made in his image.

A Biography Bibliography

This bibliography scratches the surface of all that is available. Below are some biographies that have made a major impact on my own life.

Anderson, Courtney. *To the Golden Shore: The Life of Adoniram Judson*. Toronto, Canada: Judson Press, 1956.

Augustine. *Confessions*. New York: Penguin, 1961.

Bennett, Tyler. *The Life and Labors of Asahel Nettleton*. Carlisle, PA: Banner of Truth, 1996.

Bonar, Andrew. *The Memoirs and Remains of Robert Murray M'Cheyne*. Carlisle, PA: Banner of Truth, 1987.

Cook, Faith. *The Nine Day Queen of England, Lady Jane Grey*. Darlington, UK: Evangelical Press, 2004.

Dallimore, Arnold. *A Heart Set Free: The Life of Charles Wesley*. Darlington, UK: Evangelical Press, 1988.

_____. *The Life and Times of George Whitefield*. 2 vols. Carlisle, PA: Banner of Truth, 1980.

_____. *Spurgeon: A New Biography*. Carlisle, PA: Banner of Truth, 1984.

Daniell, David. *William Tyndale: A Biography*. New Haven; London: Yale University Press, 1994.

Dodds, Elisabeth. *Marriage to a Difficult Man: The Uncommon Union of Jonathan and Sarah Edwards*. Laurel, MS: Audobon Press, 2005.

Edwards, Jonathan. *The Diary and Journal of David Brainerd*. Carlisle, PA: Banner of Truth, 2007.

Elliot, Elisabeth. *Shadow of the Almighty: The Life and Testament of Jim Elliot*. San Francisco: Harper & Row, 1989.

Glover, A. E. *1000 Miles of Miracle*. Ross-shire, UK: Christian Focus, 2000.

James, Sharon. *In Trouble and in Joy*. Darlington, UK: Evangelical Press, 2003.

_____. *My Heart in His Hands: Ann Judson of Burma*. Darlington, UK: Evangelical Press, 1998.

Murray, Iain. *Jonathan Edwards: A New Biography*. Carlisle, PA: Banner of Truth, 1987.

Paton, John G. *John G. Paton, Missionary to the New Hebrides.* Carlisle, PA; Banner of Truth, 1965.

Piper, John. *Contending for Our All: Defending Truth and Treasuring Christ in the Lives of Athanasius, John Owen, and J. Gresham Machen.* Wheaton, IL: Crossway, 2006.

——. *The Hidden Smile of God: The Fruit of Affliction in the Lives of John Bunyan, William Cowper, and David Brainerd.* Wheaton, IL: Crossway, 2001.

——. *The Legacy of Sovereign Joy: God's Triumphant Grace in the Lives of Augustine, Luther, and Calvin.* Wheaton, IL: Crossway, 2000.

——. *The Roots of Endurance: Invincible Perseverance in the Lives of John Newton, Charles Simeon, and William Wilberforce.* Wheaton, IL: Crossway, 2002.

Piper, Noël. *Faithful Women and Their Extraordinary God.* Wheaton, IL: Crossway, 2005.

Purves, Jock. *Fair Sunshine.* Carlisle, PA: Banner of Truth, 1991.

Thornbury, John. *God Sent Revival: Asahel Nettleton.* Darlington, UK: Evangelical Press, 1988.

Bibliography

Allen, Ronald B. *And I Will Praise Him: A Guide to Worship in the Psalms*. Nashville, TN: Thomas Nelson, 1992.

Allender, Dan, and Tremper Longman. *The Cry of the Soul*. Colorado Springs, CO: NavPress, 1994.

Andrews, Jim. *Polishing God's Monuments*. Wapwallopen, PA: Shepherd Press, 2007.

Benner, D. G. "Emotion." In *Evangelical Dictionary of Theology*, edited by Walter Elwell. Grand Rapids, MI: Baker, 1996.

Blaikie, William G., and Robert Law. *Glimpses of the Inner Life of Our Lord and The Emotions of Jesus*, 1876. Reprint, Stoke-on-Trent, Staffs: Tentmaker Publications, 1995.

Blomberg, Craig. *Interpreting the Parables*. Downers Grove, IL: InterVarsity, 1990.

Bonhoeffer, Dietrich. *Life Together*. San Francisco: Harper & Row, 1954.

Borgman, Brian. "Jesus, Man as Man Ought to Be." Sermon, Hebrews 2:5–8a, January 28, 2007.

———. *My Heart for Thy Cause*. Ross-shire, UK: Christian Focus, 2002.

———. "Rethinking a Much Abused Text: 1 Corinthians 3:1–15." *Reformation and Revival Journal*, 11, no. 1 (2002): 69–91.

Boston, Thomas. *Human Nature in Its Fourfold State*. Reprint, Edinburgh: Banner of Truth, 1964.

Bridges, Charles. *The Christian Ministry*, 1830. Reprint, Edinburgh: Banner of Truth, 1959.

Bridges, Jerry. *The Pursuit of Holiness*. Colorado Springs, CO: NavPress, 1978.

———. *Trusting God*. Colorado Springs, CO: NavPress, 1988.

Broger, John C. *Self-Confrontation: A Manual for In-Depth Biblical Discipleship*. Palm Desert, CA: Biblical Counseling Foundation, 1991 edition.

Carson, D. A. *The Difficult Doctrine of the Love of God*. Wheaton, IL: Crossway, 2000.

———. *The Gospel according to* John. Leicester: Inter-Varsity; Grand Rapids, MI: Eerdmans, 1991.

———. *How Long, O Lord? Reflections on Suffering and Evil*. Grand Rapids, MI: Baker, 1990, 2006.

———. "Matthew." In *The Expositor's Bible Commentary*. Vol. 8. Grand Rapids, MI: Zondervan, 1984.

Dabney, Robert L. *Discussions: Evangelical and Theological*. Vol. 2, 1891. Reprint, Edinburgh: Banner of Truth, 1967.

DeMoss, Nancy Leigh. *Choosing Forgiveness*. Chicago: Moody, 2006.

Edwards, Jonathan. *Charity and Its Fruits*, 1852. Reprint, Edinburgh: Banner of Truth, 1969.

————. *The Religious Affections*, 1746. Reprint, Edinburgh: Banner of Truth, 1961.

————. *The Works of Jonathan Edwards*. Vols. 1 and 2, 1834. Reprint, Edinburgh: Banner of Truth, 1974.

Elliott, Matthew A. *Faithful Feelings: Rethinking Emotion in the New Testament*. Grand Rapids, MI: Kregel, 2006.

Fitzpatrick, Elyse, and Laura Hendrickson. *Will Medicine Stop the Pain?* Chicago: Moody, 2006.

Fraser, James. *A Treatise on Sanctification*, 1774. Reprint, Audubon, NJ: Old Paths Publications, 1992.

Gilham, Bill. *Lifetime Guarantee*. Eugene, OR: Harvest, 1993.

Goldingay, John. *Psalms*. Vol. 1. Baker Book House Commentary on the Old Testament Wisdom and Psalms. Grand Rapids, MI: Baker, 2006.

Greidanus, Sydney. *The Modern Preacher and the Ancient Text*. Grand Rapids, MI: Eerdmans, 1988.

Hafemann, Scott. *2 Corinthians*. NIV Application Commentary. Grand Rapids, MI: Zondervan, 2000.

————. *The God of Promise and the Life of Faith*. Wheaton, IL: Crossway, 2001.

Hagner, Donald. *Matthew 14–28*. Word Biblical Commentary. Dallas, TX: Word, 1995.

Harris, Murray. *Second Epistle to the Corinthians*. New International Greek New Testament Commentary. Grand Rapids, MI: Eerdmans, 2005.

Hodge, Charles. *Systematic Theology*. 3 Vols., 1871. Reprint, Grand Rapids, MI: Eerdmans, 1989.

Jones, Robert D. *Uprooting Anger*. Phillipsburg, NJ: P&R, 2005.

Kistemaker, Simon. *The Parables of Jesus*. Grand Rapids, MI: Baker, 1980.

Lane, William. *Hebrews 1–8*. Word Biblical Commentary. Dallas, TX: Word, 1991.

Lewis, C. S. *Reflections on the Psalms*, 1958. Copyright renewed, San Diego; New York; London: Harcourt Brace, 1986.

Lloyd-Jones, D. Martyn. *Spiritual Depression: Its Causes and Its Cure*. Grand Rapids, MI: Eerdmans, 1965.

Longman, Tremper. *Reading the Bible with Heart and Mind*. Colorado Springs, CO: Navpress, 1997.

Lundgaard, Kris. *Through the Looking Glass*. Phillipsburg, NJ: P&R, 2000.

Machen, J. Gresham. *Christianity and Liberalism*. Grand Rapids, MI: Eerdmans, 1923.

_____. *God Transcendent*. Grand Rapids, MI: Eerdmans, 1949. Reprint, Edinburgh: Banner of Truth, 1982.

Mack, Wayne. *Out of the Blues: Dealing with the Blues of Depression and Loneliness*. Bemidjii, MN: Focus Publishing, 2006.

Macleod, Donald. *Behold Your God*. Scotland: Christian Focus, 1995.

Manton, Thomas. *James*, 1693. Reprint, Edinburgh: Banner of Truth, 1962.

Martin, Albert N. "Jesus Christ: Pattern for Our Emotional Life." Sermon series, Trinity Pulpit. http://www.tbcnj.org.

Morris, Leon. *The Gospel according to Matthew*. Pillar New Testament Commentary. Grand Rapids, MI: Eerdmans, 1992.

Motyer, J. Alec. *The Message of James*. Downers Grove, IL: InterVarsity, 1985.

_____. *The Prophecy of Isaiah*. Downers Grove, IL: InterVarsity, 1993.

Murphy, Thomas. *Pastoral Theology*, 1877. Reprint, Audubon, NJ: Old Paths Publications, 1996.

Murray, Iain. "The Life of John Murray." Vol. 3. *The Collected Writings of John Murray*. Edinburgh: Banner of Truth, 1982.

Murray, John. *The Collected Writings*. Vol. 2. Edinburgh: Banner of Truth, 1978.

Nichols, Gregory G. "The Emotivity of God." *Reformed Baptist Theological Review*, 1 no. 2 (July 2004): 95–143.

Owen, John. *The Glory of Christ*. Abridged by R. J. K. Law. Edinburgh: Banner of Truth, 1994.

_____. *Overcoming Sin and Temptation*. Edited by Kelly Kapic and Justin Taylor. Wheaton, IL: Crossway, 2006.

_____. *Sin and Grace*. Vol. 7. Goold edition, 1850–1853. Reprint, Edinburgh: Banner of Truth, 1965.

_____. *Temptation and Sin*. Vol. 6. Goold edition, 1850–1853. Reprint, Edinburgh: Banner of Truth, 1967.

Packer, J. I. *Knowing God*. Downers Grove, IL: InterVarsity, 1973.

Packer, J. I., and Carol Nystrom. *Praying: Finding Our Way through Duty to Delight*. Downers Grove, IL: InterVarsity, 2006.

Pink, A. W. *The Attributes of God*. Grand Rapids, MI: Baker, 1990.

_____. *The Sovereignty of God*, 1928. Reprint, Edinburgh: Banner of Truth, 1961.

Piper, John. "As We Have also Forgiven Our Debtors." Sermon, March 20, 1994. http://www.desiringgod.org.

_____. "Battling Unbelief at Bethlehem." Sermon, September 11, 1988. http://www.desiringgod.org.

_____. "Battling the Unbelief of Bitterness." Sermon, November 20, 1988. http://www.desiringgod.org.

_____. *Brothers, We Are Not Professionals*. Nashville, TN: Broadman and Holman, 2002.

_____. *Counted Righteous in Christ*. Wheaton, IL: Crossway, 2002.

_____. *Desiring God*. Portland, OR: Multnomah, 1986, 1996, 2003.

_____. *Future Grace*. Sisters, OR: Multnomah, 1995.

_____. *The Future of Justification*. Wheaton, IL: Crossway, 2007.

_____. *The Pleasures of God*. Portland, OR: Multnomah, 1991.

_____. *The Supremacy of God in Preaching*. Grand Rapids, MI: Baker, 1990.

_____. "The Value of Relationships: Fresh Initiatives for the Immediate Future of Our Mission." Sermon, November 19, 1995. http://www.desiring-god.org.

_____. *When the Darkness Will Not Lift: Doing What We Can While We Wait for God—and Joy*. Wheaton, IL: Crossway, 2006.

Pond, Clifford. *The Beauty of Jesus*. London: Grace Publications, 1994.

Powlison, David. *Seeing with New Eyes*. Phillipsburg, NJ: P&R, 2003.

Priolo, Lou. *The Heart of Anger*. Amityville, NY: Calvary Press, 1997.

Rayburn, Robert. "Preaching as Mystical Event." Lecture delivered at the Banner of Truth Ministers Conference, May 29–31, 2001.

Reymond, Robert. *A New Systematic Theology of the Christian Faith*. Nashville, TN: Thomas Nelson, 1998.

Ryle, J. C. *Expository Thoughts on the Gospels*. Vol. 2. Reprint, Grand Rapids, MI: Zondervan, 1951.

_____. *Holiness*, 1879. Reprint, Durham, England: Evangelical Press, 1979.

Spurgeon, Charles. *Lectures to My Students*, 1881. Reprint, Pasadena, TX: Pilgrim, 1990.

Stalker, James. *Imago Christi*, 1889. Reprint, Birmingham, AL: Solid Ground Christian Books, 2003.

Storms, Sam. "Joy's Eternal Increase: Edwards on the Beauty of Heaven." Talk delivered at Desiring God 2003 National Conference. http://www.desiring-god.org.

_____. "The Will: Fettered yet Free." In *A God-Entranced Vision of All Things: The Legacy of Jonathan Edwards*, edited by John Piper and Justin Taylor. Wheaton, IL: Crossway, 2004.

Tada, Joni Eareckson. *When God Weeps*. Grand Rapids, MI: Zondervan, 1997.

Talbot, Mark R. "Godly Emotions (*Religious Affections*)." In *A God-Entranced Vision of All Things, The Legacy of Jonathan Edwards*, edited by John Piper and Justin Taylor. Wheaton, IL: Crossway, 2004.

Tozer, A. W. *The Knowledge of the Holy*. San Francisco: Harper & Row, 1961.

Tripp, Paul. *Instruments in the Redeemer's Hands*. Phillipsburg, NJ: P&R, 2002.

Venema, Cornelius. *Getting the Gospel Right*. Edinburgh: Banner of Truth, 2006.

Ware, Bruce A. *God's Greater Glory*. Wheaton, IL: Crossway, 2004.

Warfield, B. B. *The Person and Work of Christ*. Philadelphia, PA: Presbyterian and Reformed, 1950.

———. *The Savior of the World*, 1916. Reprint, Edinburgh: Banner of Truth, 1991.

Waters, Guy. *Justification and the New Perspective on Paul: A Review and Response*. Phillipsburg, NJ: P&R, 2004.

Welch, Edward T. *Addictions: A Banquet in the Grave*. Phillipsburg, NJ: P&R, 2001.

———. *Blame It on the Brain: Distinguishing Chemical Imbalances, Brain Disorders, and Disobedience*. Phillipsburg, NJ: P&R, 1998.

———. *When People Are Big and God Is Small*. Phillipsburg, NJ: P&R, 1997.

———. *Depression: A Stubborn Darkness*. Winston-Salem, NC: Punch Press, 2004.

Williams, Sam. "Toward a Theology of Emotion." *Southern Baptist Theological Journal*, 7, no. 4 (Winter 2003): 58–73.

Notes

Introduction

1. Matthew A. Elliott, *Faithful Feelings: Rethinking Emotion in the New Testament* (Grand Rapids, MI: Kregel, 2006), 12.
2. D. Martyn Lloyd-Jones, *Spiritual Depression: Its Causes and Its Cure* (Grand Rapids, MI: Eerdmans, 1965), 109.
3. http://www.emotionsanonymous.org/.
4. Bill Gilham, *Lifetime Guarantee* (Eugene, OR: Harvest, 1993), 149.
5. Elliott, *Faithful Feelings*, 16–55.
6. Mark R. Talbot, "Godly Emotions (*Religious Affections*)," in *A God-Entranced Vision of All Things: The Legacy of Jonathan Edwards*, ed. John Piper and Justin Taylor (Wheaton, IL: Crossway, 2004), 235.
7. Elliott, *Faithful Feelings*, 54.
8. At a psychological and perhaps even a theological level, the emotions, feelings, and affections could be differentiated. Emotions begin in the mind. Emotions produce feelings and are experienced in the body. But the way I use the term *emotions* throughout will have obvious overlap with *feelings* and *affections*. For an attempt to distinguish these categories see Sam Williams, "Toward a Theology of Emotion," *Southern Baptist Theological Journal*, 7, no. 4 (Winter 2003): 59–61.
9. D. G. Benner, "Emotion," in *Evangelical Dictionary of Theology*, ed. Walter Elwell (Grand Rapids, MI: Baker, 1996), 353.
10. Dan Allender and Tremper Longman, *The Cry of the Soul* (Colorado Springs, CO: Navpress, 1994), 25. Although this book is filled with many good insights, I believe it has certain theological and biblical deficiencies.
11. Sam Williams, "Toward a Theology of Emotion," 66.

Chapter 1: The Character of God

1. A.W. Tozer, *The Knowledge of the Holy* (San Francisco: Harper & Row, 1961), 6.
2. Matthew A. Elliott, *Faithful Feelings: Rethinking Emotion in the New Testament* (Grand Rapids, MI: Kregel, 2006), 105.
3. Appendix 1 addresses the doctrine of impassibility.
4. Gregory G. Nichols, "Doctrine of God, Part 3: The Nature of God," section 2, unit 8, lecture 15 (Fall 1997). All further quotations are from this section of his lecture. Since I preached this series, Nichols's material has been published in *Reformed Baptist Theological Review*, 1, no. 2 (July 2004): 95–143. It is an excellent study.
5. Elliott, *Faithful Feelings*, 111.
6. B. B. Warfield, *The Savior of the World* (1916; repr., Edinburgh: Banner of Truth, 1991), 117.
7. The servant songs are Isa. 42:1–9; 49:1–6; 50:4–9; 52:13–53:12.
8. John Piper, *The Pleasures of God* (Portland, OR: Multnomah, 1991), 38.
9. "Who Am I?" Casting Crowns; words and music by Mark Hall.

10. The NASB reads, "He will be quiet in His love."
11. See appendix 1 on divine impassibility.
12. NASB: "how I have been hurt by their adulterous hearts."
13. Elliott, *Faithful Feelings*, 109.
14. J. Alec Motyer, *The Prophecy of Isaiah* (Downers Grove, IL: InterVarsity, 1993), 394.
15. Elliott, *Faithful Feelings*, 111.

Chapter 2: The Character of the Word

1. B. B. Warfield, "On Emotional Life of Our Lord," in *The Person and Work of Christ* (Philadelphia, PA: Presbyterian and Reformed, 1950), 93.
2. Bill Gilham, *Lifetime Guarantee* (Eugene, OR: Harvest, 1993), 149.
3. D. G. Benner, "Emotion," in *Evangelical Dictionary of Theology*, ed. Walter Elwell (Grand Rapids, MI: Baker, 1996), 352.
4. Jonathan Edwards, *The Religious Affections* (1746; repr., Edinburgh: Banner of Truth, 1961), 52–53.

Chapter 3: A Biblical Anthropology

1. Dan Allender and Tremper Longman, *The Cry of the Soul* (Colorado Springs, CO: Navpress, 1994), 39.
2. Thomas Boston, *Human Nature in Its Fourfold State* (repr., Edinburgh: Banner of Truth, 1964), 40–43.
3. See also Sam Williams, "Toward a Theology of Emotion," *Southern Baptist Theological Journal*, 7, no. 4 (Winter 2003) and his discussion on the pre-fall capacity for emotion in Adam and Eve, 65.
4. For an excellent treatment of Edwards's work on the will see Sam Storms, "The Will: Fettered Yet Free," in *A God-Entranced Vision of All Things: The Legacy of Jonathan Edwards*, ed. John Piper and Justin Taylor (Wheaton, IL: Crossway, 2004), 201–20.
5. Boston, *Human Nature in Its Fourfold State*, 127.
6. See Sam Williams, "Toward a Theology of Emotion," 68.
7. Mark R. Talbot, "Godly Emotions (*Religious Affections*)," in *A God-Entranced Vision of All Things*, 230, 234.
8. "Regeneration and sanctification don't necessarily make us any more emotional, although they certainly are intended to renew our emotions and kindle and redirect the affections so that, in increasing measures, the new man is able to love God and neighbor more wholeheartedly and to hate evil and sin" (Sam Williams, "Toward a Theology of Emotion," 70).
9. "Praise the Savior, Ye Who Know Him," #677, *Trinity Hymnal*, rev. (Atlanta, GA: Great Commission Publications, 1990).
10. Jonathan Edwards, *Charity and Its Fruits* (1852; repr., Edinburgh: Banner of Truth, 1969), 327–28, 331–32.
11. See ibid., 335–36, and also see the masterful essay/lecture by Sam Storms, "Joy's Eternal Increase: Edwards on the Beauty of Heaven," Desiring God 2003 National Conference, http://www.desiringgod.org.

Chapter 4: The Authority of God's Word

1. Bill Gilham, *Lifetime Guarantee* (Eugene, OR: Harvest, 1993), 149.
2. John C. Broger, *Self-Confrontation: A Manual for In-Depth Biblical Discipleship* (Palm Desert, CA: Biblical Counseling Foundation, 1991 ed.), 325; italics original.

3. D. Martyn Lloyd-Jones, *Spiritual Depression: Its Causes and Its Cure* (Grand Rapids, MI: Eerdmans, 1965), 101.
4. John Piper, *Desiring God* (Portland, OR: Multnomah, 1986, 1996, 2003), 299–301. The whole book supports, defends, and expounds the central role of the emotions or affections.

Chapter 5: The Foundation and Priority of Truth

1. D. Martyn Lloyd-Jones, *Spiritual Depression: Its Causes and Its Cure* (Grand Rapids, MI: Eerdmans, 1965), 61.
2. Dan Allender and Tremper Longman, *The Cry of the Soul* (Colorado Springs, CO: Navpress, 1994), 16.
3. Bruce A. Ware, *God's Greater Glory* (Wheaton, IL: Crossway, 2004), 15.
4. A.W. Tozer, *The Knowledge of the Holy* (San Francisco: Harper & Row, 1961), 1.
5. A.W. Pink, *The Sovereignty of God* (1928; repr., Edinburgh: Banner of Truth, 1961), 16.
6. A.W. Pink, *The Attributes of God* (Grand Rapids, MI: Baker, 1991), Preface.
7. Scott Hafemann, *The God of Promise and the Life of Faith* (Wheaton, IL: Crossway, 2001), 168, 184.
8. Italics added.
9. Others have done this far more effectively than I could. See, for example, John Piper, *Counted Righteous in Christ* (Wheaton, IL: Crossway, 2002); *The Future of Justification* (Wheaton, IL: Crossway, 2007); Guy Waters, *Justification and the New Perspective on Paul: A Review and Response* (Phillipsburg, NJ: P&R, 2004); Cornelius Venema, *Getting the Gospel Right* (Edinburgh: Banner of Truth, 2006).
10. For an excellent treatment of Christ's active obedience, see John Murray, *The Collected Writings*, vol. 2 (Edinburgh: Banner of Truth, 1978). What follows comes from his work on the subject.
11. Jesus' learning obedience does not imply moral defect. Heb. 4:15 and 7:26 clearly assert his sinlessness.
12. For instance, J. Gresham Machen, *God Transcendent* (Grand Rapids, MI: Eerdmans, 1949; repr., Edinburgh: Banner of Truth, 1982), 190–91.
13. Donald Macleod, *Behold Your God* (Ross-shire, UK: Christian Focus, 1995), 106.
14. Hafemann, *The God of Promise*, 167.

Chapter 6: A Theology of Christian Experience

1. See my article "Rethinking a Much Abused Text: 1 Corinthians 3:1–15," in *Reformation and Revival Journal*, 11, no. 1 (2002): 69–91, for an exegetical assessment and the dangers of this view.
2. John Owen, *Sin and Temptation*, vol. 6 (Edinburgh: Banner of Truth, 1967; and other editions); J. C. Ryle, *Holiness* (1879; repr., Durham, England: Evangelical Press, 1979); Jerry Bridges, *The Pursuit of Holiness* (Colorado Springs, CO: Navpress, 1978); John Murray, *Collected Writings*, vol. 2 (Edinburgh: Banner of Truth, 1978). I would also add the more difficult-to-find *A Treatise on Sanctification* by James Fraser (1774; repr., Audubon, NJ: Old Paths, 1992).
3. D. A. Carson, *How Long O Lord? Reflections on Suffering and Evil* (Grand Rapids, MI: Baker, 1990, 2006); Jerry Bridges, *Trusting God* (Colorado Springs, CO: NavPress, 1988); Joni Eareckson Tada, *When God Weeps* (Grand Rapids, MI:

Zondervan, 1997); Jim Andrews, *Polishing God's Monuments* (Wapwallopen, PA: Shepherd Press, 2007).

4. I want to qualify this by acknowledging that gladness is not just happiness or unfettered joy. There may be times of grief or sorrow that temper our gladness. However, the exceptions do not nullify the rule.

Chapter 7: How to Handle the Emotions

1. Scott Hafemann, *The God of Promise and the Life of Faith* (Wheaton, IL: Crossway, 2001), 184; italics added.
2. Mark R. Talbot, "Godly Emotions (*Religious Affections*)," in *A God-Entranced Vision of All Things: The Legacy of Jonathan Edwards*, ed. John Piper and Justin Taylor (Wheaton, IL: Crossway, 2004), 254.
3. Ronald B. Allen, *And I Will Praise Him: A Guide to Worship in the Psalms* (Nashville: Thomas Nelson, 1992), 17.
4. C. S. Lewis, *Reflections on the Psalms* (1958; repr., San Diego: Harcourt Brace, 1986), 3.
5. John Goldingay, *Psalms*, vol. 1, Baker Book House Commentary on the Old Testament Wisdom and Psalms (Grand Rapids, MI: Baker, 2006), 137.
6. Ibid., 138.
7. Ibid., 134.
8. Ibid., 139; italics added.
9. Ibid., 232.
10. John Piper, *Brothers, We Are Not Professionals* (Nashville, TN: Broadman and Holman, 2002), 146.
11. Scott Hafemann, *2 Corinthians*, NIV Application Commentary (Grand Rapids, MI: Zondervan, 2000), 64.
12. Murray Harris, *Second Epistle to the Corinthians*, NIGNTC (Grand Rapids, MI: Eerdmans, 2005), 158.
13. Dan Allender and Tremper Longman, *The Cry of the Soul* (Colorado Springs, CO: NavPress, 1994), 26–27.
14. See the excellent work by Jim Andrews, *Polishing God's Monuments: Pillars of Hope for Punishing Times* (Wapwallopen, PA: Shepherd Press, 2007).

Chapter 8: Mortifying Ungodly Emotions

1. D. Martyn Lloyd-Jones, *Spiritual Depression: Its Causes and Its Cure* (Grand Rapids, MI: Eerdmans, 1965), 16–17.
2. Thomas Manton, *James* (1693; repr., Edinburgh: Banner of Truth, 1962), 457.
3. Dietrich Bonhoeffer, *Life Together* (San Francisco: Harper & Row, 1954), 112.
4. I am indebted to far more people in these case studies than I can possibly remember. Although I will try to document all appropriate sources, my recollection may be sketchy in some instances.

Chapter 9: Sinful Anger

1. Robert D. Jones, *Uprooting Anger* (Phillipsburg, NJ: P&R, 2005), 15.
2. Lou Priolo, *The Heart of Anger* (Amityville, NY: Calvary Press, 1997), 81.
3. Alec Motyer, *The Message of James* (Downers Grove, IL: InterVarsity, 1985), 66.
4. Paul Tripp, *Instruments in the Redeemer's Hands* (Phillipsburg, NJ: P&R, 2002), 77.
5. Tripp, *Instruments*, 79.
6. Jones, *Uprooting Anger*, 100.
7. Dietrich Bonhoeffer, *Life Together* (San Francisco: Harper & Row, 1954), 74.

8. Priolo, *The Heart of Anger*, 79–89.

Chapter 10: Unforgiveness and Bitterness

1. Nancy Leigh DeMoss, *Choosing Forgiveness* (Chicago, IL: Moody, 2006), 56.
2. Simon Kistemaker, *The Parables of Jesus* (Grand Rapids, MI: Baker, 1980), 66.
3. Leon Morris, *The Gospel according to Matthew*, A Pillar Commentary (Grand Rapids, MI: Eerdmans, 1992), 473–74.
4. D. A. Carson, "Matthew," in *The Expositor's Bible Commentary*, vol. 8 (Grand Rapids, MI: Zondervan, 1984), 407.
5. Craig Blomberg, *Interpreting the Parables* (Downers Grove, IL: InterVarsity, 1990), 242.
6. D. A. Carson, "Matthew," 407.
7. Donald Hagner, *Matthew 14–28*, Word Biblical Commentary (Dallas, TX: Word, 1995), 536.
8. I understand Nancy DeMoss's qualification that feelings don't prove forgiveness. But I do take *some* exception to her statement, "Forgiveness is a choice, feelings are not" (p. 171). Although forgiveness is more than feelings, we cannot ignore the emotional element in "forgive from the heart." This does not mean that every time I have an unforgiving feeling I am unforgiving, but the feelings must be dealt with through truth.
9. "As We Have Also Forgiven Our Debtors," sermon, March 20, 1994, http://www.desiringgod.org.
10. This last point is very important. Some teach you do not forgive until the offender asks for forgiveness and repents. However, in the court of heaven, through prayer, we can forgive people of their sins against us. I believe this is necessary if we are to be free of an unforgiving spirit and bitterness. Nevertheless, there is incompleteness in the process and no reconciliation until the offender seeks forgiveness.
11. DeMoss, *Choosing Forgiveness*, 28.
12. "Battling the Unbelief of Bitterness," sermon, November 20, 1988, http://www.desiringgod.org.

Chapter 11: Fear, Anxiety, and Worry

1. Dan Allender and Tremper Longman, *The Cry of the Soul* (Colorado Springs, CO: Navpress, 1994), 80.
2. For an outstanding treatment of the fear of man, see Edward T. Welch, *When People Are Big and God Is Small* (Phillipsburg, NJ: P&R, 1997).
3. David Powlison, *Seeing with New Eyes* (Phillipsburg, NJ: P&R, 2003), 115.
4. John Piper, *Future Grace* (Sisters, OR: Multnomah, 1995), 53.
5. John Goldingay thinks, "The declaration that Yhwh is my light is characteristically spelled out as implying that Yhwh is deliverer." *Psalms*, vol. 1, Baker Book House Commentary on the Old Testament Wisdom and Psalms (Grand Rapids, MI: Baker, 2006), 392.

Chapter 12: Depression

1. For a fuller treatment, see Wayne Mack, *Out of the Blues: Dealing with the Blues of Depression and Loneliness* (Bemidjii, MN: Focus, 2006); Ed Welch, *Depression: A Stubborn Darkness* (Winston-Salem, NC: Punch, 2004); John Piper, *When the Darkness Will Not Lift: Doing What We Can While We Wait for God—*

and Joy (Wheaton, IL: Crossway, 2006); and D. Martyn Lloyd-Jones, *Spiritual Depression: Its Causes and Its Cure* (Grand Rapids, MI: Eerdmans, 1965).

2. Ed Welch, *Depression*, 166–67.
3. See Ed Welch, *Blame It on the Brain?* (Phillipsburg, NJ: P&R, 1998), 120, fig. 7.2.
4. I would suggest that the spiritual and physical fatigue Elijah had experienced in 1 Kings 18 contributed to his depressed state in 1 Kings 19.
5. Welch, *Blame It on the Brain?* 122.
6. For example, hyperthyroidism and mineral and vitamin deficiencies.
7. John C. Broeger, *Self-Confrontation: A Manual for In-Depth Biblical Discipleship* (Palm Desert, CA: Biblical Counseling Foundation, 1991 ed.), 322.
8. I would highly recommend Elyse Fitzpatrick and Laura Hendrickson, *Will Medicine Stop the Pain?* (Chicago: Moody, 2006). Chapter 2 and Appendices B and C deal specifically with medication.
9. See Welch's treatment of addiction as idolatry, pp. 47–55.
10. Welch, *Blame It on the Brain?* 123.
11. We should also learn to sing the truths to ourselves. A good hymnal can be a powerful weapon in the fight against depression and bring comfort to the soul. We will explore the role of singing and the emotions in chapter 16.
12. Welch, *Depression*, 97.
13. Lloyd-Jones, *Spiritual Depression*, 20–21.

Chapter 13: Cultivating Godly Emotions

1. Sam Williams, "Toward a Theology of Emotion," *Southern Baptist Theological Journal*, 7, no. 4 (Winter 2003): 72.
2. See Albert N. Martin's excellent four-part sermon series "Jesus Christ: Pattern for Our Emotional Life," available from Trinity Baptist Church, Montville, NJ, http://www.tbcnj.org.

Chapter 14: Jesus Our Pattern, Part 1

1. See my sermon "Jesus, Man as Man Ought to Be" (Heb. 2:5–8a), January 28, 2007, for a defense of Heb. 2:5–8 as focusing on Christ, http://www.gracenevada.com.
2. B. B. Warfield, "On the Emotional Life of Our Lord," in *The Person and Work of Christ* (Philadelphia, PA: Presbyterian and Reformed, 1950), 93.
3. I object to the translation, "new *self*" (ESV, NASB, NIV) or "new *nature*" (RSV) because the "new man" here is probably a redemptive-historical reference to Christ (cf. Eph. 4:24).
4. Clifford Pond, *The Beauty of Jesus* (London: Grace Publications, 1994), 52.
5. William G. Blaikie and Robert Law, *Glimpses of the Inner Life of Our Lord and the Emotions of Jesus* (1876; repr., Tentmaker Publications, 1995). Since this book is actually two in one, each with its own page numbers, I will note, here and following, the author and the page number: Blaikie, 13.
6. B. B. Warfield, "Emotional Life," 126. See also Blaikie, chap. 9; Law, chap. 1; Pond, chap. 13.
7. Blaikie, *Glimpses of the Inner Life of Our Lord*, 15.
8. Warfield, "Emotional Life," 123–24, 126.
9. Quoted in John Piper, *Desiring God* (Portland, OR: Multnomah, 1986, 1996, 2003), 20.
10. I would argue this is the point of Ecclesiastes. Although life is a mystery, it is the gift of God. Once we see life as a gift we are equipped to enjoy it in

spite of the mystery. Ecclesiastes teaches us to glorify God by trusting him with the enigmas and enjoying this fleeting life.

11. Dietrich Bonhoeffer, *Life Together* (San Francisco: Harper & Row, 1954), 67.

Chapter 15: Jesus Our Pattern, Part 2

1. B. B. Warfield, "On the Emotional Life of Our Lord," in *The Person and Work of Christ* (Philadelphia: Presbyterian and Reformed, 1950), 96.
2. In the OT, *racham* is a word derived from "womb" or "belly," denoting a deep, inner feeling. In the NT, *splagnizomai* and its cognates denote the feeling of sympathy in the inward parts, the entrails, which were seen to be the seat of the emotions. The two words are parallel.
3. In the OT, *chamal* focuses on the action of showing mercy. In the NT, there is *oiktirō* and cognates of *patheō*, which focus on showing compassion, sensitivity, and gentleness.
4. James Stalker, *Imago Christi* (1889; repr., Birmingham, AL: Solid Ground Christian Books, 2003), 303.
5. Warfield, "Emotional Life," 100.
6. Ibid., 101.
7. Clifford Pond, *The Beauty of Jesus* (London: Grace Publications, 1994), 70–87, shows how Jesus fulfills each of these descriptions.
8. J. C. Ryle, *Expository Thoughts on the Gospels*, vol. 2 (Grand Rapids, MI: Zondervan, 1951), 463.
9. "In My Heart," words and music, Eric Grover.
10. Grover, "In My Heart."
11. This section owes a great deal to Cliff Pond and his insights from chapter 19, "Perfect Symmetry," in *The Beauty of Jesus.*
12. Ibid., 117. See also chap. 3, "A Biblical Anthropology."
13. Stalker, *Imago Christi*, 305.
14. William G. Blaikie and Robert Law, *Glimpses of the Inner Life of Our Lord and the Emotions of Jesus* (1876; repr., Tentmaker Publications, 1995), Law: 49.
15. E.g., John Owen, *The Glory of Christ*, abridged R. J. K. Law (Edinburgh: Banner of Truth, 1994); Kris Lundgaard, *Through the Looking Glass* (Phillipsburg, NJ: P&R, 2000); and Jonathan Edwards, "The Excellency of Christ," in *The Works of Jonathan Edwards*, vol. 1 (1834; repr., Edinburgh: Banner of Truth, 1974), 680–89.
16. Owen, *The Glory of Christ*, 7.

Chapter 16: Renewing Our Minds

1. The Greek words *nous, phronēma, phronēsis, phroneō, logizomai*, and *logismos* are all used with regularity, and even a casual look at these words in a standard lexicon bears out the above semantic range.
2. "Have this attitude in yourselves which was also in Christ Jesus" (NASB).
3. John Frame explains the interplay: "God gives us multiple faculties to serve as a sort of internal system of checks and balances. Sometimes reason saves us from emotional craziness, but emotions can also check the extravagant pretenses of reason. . . . [Sometimes] feeling guides my reflection; my reflection refines my feelings. Those refined feelings provoke additional reflection, and so on. The goal is a satisfying analysis, an analysis I feel good about, one with which I have cognitive rest, a peaceful relation between

intellect and emotion." Quoted in Sam Williams, "Toward a Theology of Emotion," *Southern Baptist Theological Journal*, 7, no. 4 (Winter 2003): 69.

Matthew Elliott also states, "Emotions are a key element in learning, communication, ethics, and behavior" (*Faithful Feelings: Rethinking Emotion in the New Testament* [Grand Rapids, MI: Kregel, 2006], 239).

4. It is my sincere hope that volume 7 is made more accessible to modern readers, just as volume 6 has been in editions like *Overcoming Sin and Temptation*, ed. Kelly Kapic and Justin Taylor (Wheaton, IL: Crossway, 2006).

5. John Owen, "The Grace and Duty of Being Spiritually Minded," in *The Works of John Owen*, vol. 7 (Edinburgh: Banner of Truth, 1965), 275.

6. Elliott, *Faithful Feelings*, 252.

Chapter 17: The Emotions and Worship

1. "Both the Pietist and the rationalist separate emotion and thinking, one emphasizing one and one the other. They make the same mistake." (Matthew Elliott, *Faithful Feelings: Rethinking Emotion in the New Testament* [Grand Rapids, MI: Kregel, 2006], 257).

2. The Psalms are poetry, but they were also written in meter to be sung, as many of the superscriptions indicate.

3. Many New Testament scholars believe that such passages as Phil. 2:6–11; Col. 1:15–20; and 1 Tim. 3:16 were originally hymns written in honor of Christ. Paul may have been the original author or he may have used the well-known words, much like a modern preacher would use lines from well-known hymns in a sermon.

4. The word *soul* (NASB) is *kabod*, which is usually translated "glory" (so KJV, ESV), but the word is also translated many times to refer to the inner man, thus the NASB, "soul," and the NIV, "heart."

5. Jonathan Edwards, *The Religious Affections* (1746; repr., Edinburgh: Banner of Truth, 1961), 44; italics added.

6. A. W. Tozer comments, "Worship is pure or base as the worshiper entertains high or low thoughts of God. . . . We tend by a secret law of the soul to move toward our mental image of God" (*The Knowledge of the Holy* [San Francisco: Harper & Row, 1961], 1).

7. D. A. Carson, *The Gospel according to John* (Leicester: Inter-Varsity; Grand Rapids, MI: Eerdmans, 1991), 225.

8. Christ also sings in the midst of his people. See Heb. 2:11–13; cf. Ps. 22:22.

9. Dietrich Bonhoeffer, *Life Together* (San Francisco: Harper & Row, 1954), 58.

Chapter 18: The Emotions and Preaching

1. Unfortunately, both the ESV and the NIV leave out the interjection, "Ho!" which invigorates the call with the energy of a street hawker or the peanut guy at the baseball game.

2. "The Life of John Murray," in Iain Murray, *The Collected Writings of John Murray*, vol. 3 (Edinburgh: Banner of Truth, 1982), 72.

3. Charles Spurgeon, *Lectures to My Students*, 2 (1881; repr., Pasadena, TX: Pilgrim, 1990), 147–48.

4. Thomas Murphy, *Pastoral Theology* (1877; repr., Audubon, NJ: Old Paths Publications, 1996), 191–93.

5. Charles Bridges, *The Christian Ministry* (repr., Edinburgh: Banner of Truth, 1959), 318.
6. Quoted in John Piper, *The Supremacy of God in Preaching* (Grand Rapids, MI: Baker, 1990), 84.
7. Edwards, *Religious Affections*, 44.
8. Quoted in Piper, *The Supremacy of God in Preaching*, 82–83.
9. Sydney Greidanus, *The Modern Preacher and the Ancient Text* (Grand Rapids, MI: Eerdmans, 1988), 9. See also Robert Rayburn's excellent lecture "Preaching as Mystical Event," delivered at the Banner of Truth Ministers Conference, May 29–31, 2001.
10. Quoted in Piper, *The Supremacy of God in Preaching*, 22.
11. "Some Thoughts concerning the Present Revival of Religion in New England," in *The Works of Jonathan Edwards*, vol. 1 (1834; repr., Edinburgh: Banner of Truth, 1974), 394.
12. If we take the exhortation of Heb. 4:1–2 with 4:11, then 4:12–13 is a powerful statement about the Word preached and the necessary response of obedient faith.

Chapter 19: Faith-building Relationships

1. Dietrich Bonhoeffer, *Life Together* (San Francisco: Harper & Row, 1954), 18.
2. Matthew Elliott, *Faithful Feelings: Rethinking Emotion in the New Testament* (Grand Rapids, MI: Kregel, 2006), 246.
3. Ibid., 247.
4. John Piper, "Battling Unbelief at Bethlehem," sermon, September 11, 1988, http://www.desiringgod.org.
5. William Lane, *Hebrews 1–8*, Word Biblical Commentary (Dallas, TX: Word, 1991), 87.
6. Bonhoeffer, *Life Together*, 23.
7. I would recommend, especially for pastors, John Piper's "The Value of Relationships: Fresh Initiatives for the Immediate Future of Our Mission," November 19, 1995, http://www.desiringgod.org.
8. Bonhoeffer, *Life Together*. Chapter 5 is a must-read on this subject.
9. Bryan Jeffery Leech, "We Are God's People," *Trinity Hymnal*, rev. ed. (Suwanee, GA: Great Commission Publications, 1999), #355.
10. Elliott, *Faithful Feelings*, 266.

Chapter 20: The Word and Prayer

1. Tremper Longman, *Reading the Bible with Heart and Mind* (Colorado Springs, CO: NavPress, 1997), 31.
2. John Piper, *Desiring God* (Portland, OR: Multnomah, 1986, 1996, 2003), chap. 5.
3. Scott Hafemann, *The God of Promise and the Life of Faith* (Wheaton, IL: Crossway, 2001), 183.
4. J. I. Packer and Carol Nystrom, *Praying: Finding Our Way through Duty to Delight* (Downers Grove, IL: InterVarsity, 2006), 61–62.
5. Owen, vol. 7 (Edinburgh: Banner of Truth, 1965), 284.
6. Hugh Stowell, "From Every Stormy Wind That Blows," *Trinity Hymnal*, rev. ed. (Suwanee, GA: Great Commission Publications, 1999), #631.
7. As of this draft, my mom has since been diagnosed with a brain tumor. Her faith and joy, sustained by the Word and prayer, have continued to

grow. She thanks God for this affliction because it has brought her closer to him.

Chapter 21: Reading, Meditation, and Imagination

1. This is not a condemnation of motion pictures!
2. Robert L. Dabney, *Discussions: Evangelical and Theological*, vol. 2 (1891; repr., Edinburgh: Banner of Truth, 1967, 1982), 158–69.
3. Some fiction can powerfully communicate gospel themes, which move us.
4. I am going to limit good Christian books to biography, but I wholeheartedly believe the same applies to well-written theological books.
5. John Piper, *Brothers, We Are Not Professionals* (Nashville, TN: Broadman and Holman, 2002), 90. Read the whole chapter, "Brothers, Read Christian Biography."
6. If you are new to reading Christian biography, see Appendix 2, "A Biography List," that provides some good starting places.
7. Tremper Longman, *Reading the Bible with Heart and Mind* (Colorado Springs, CO: NavPress, 1997), 33.
8. See the Longman quote above as well as the Edwards quote in chapter 2.
9. Brian Borgman, *My Heart for Thy Cause* (Ross-shire, UK: Christian Focus, 2002), 225.

Appendix 1

1. Bruce A. Ware, *God's Greater Glory* (Wheaton, IL: Crossway, 2004), 145.
2. A figure of speech related to anthropomorphism. Anthropomorphism is "the form of man," e.g., hand, eye, arm. Anthropopathism is "the feeling of man," e.g., love, hate, anger, jealousy.
3. D. A. Carson, *The Difficult Doctrine of the Love of God* (Wheaton, IL: Crossway, 2000), 59.
4. Charles Hodge, *Systematic Theology*, vol. 1 (1871; repr., Grand Rapids, MI: Eerdmans, 1989), 428–29.
5. See Elliott's helpful discussion in Matthew Elliott, *Faithful Feelings: Rethinking Emotion in the New Testament* (Grand Rapids, MI: Kregel, 2006), 105–11.
6. J. I. Packer, *Knowing God* (Downers Grove, IL: InterVarsity, 1973), 109.
7. Robert Reymond, *A New Systematic Theology of the Christian Faith* (Nashville, TN: Thomas Nelson, 1998), 179.
8. There is an element of divine mystery in how God can be immutable and sovereign, working out all things after the counsel of his will, and yet be emotionally involved with his creatures and responsive to his creatures. For a workable solution I suggest Bruce Ware's proposal of "relational mutability" and "contingent attributes" as explained in his book *God's Greater Glory*.

Subject Index

Scripture Index